More Praise for *Th* ~~on!~~

"A very rational approac ~~se you~~ wish to convince."

—Robert E. Kellar, President,
Brandywine Performance Group, Inc.

"Aubuchon proceeds, without hype, and in crisp, analytical style to unfold a detailed plan of how to make things happen. . . . If persuasion is an important element in one's line of work—and it's a rare field where it isn't—Aubuchon's book may well make the difference between success and failure."

—Richard P. Sanger,
The Prudential Preferred Properties

The
Anatomy
of
Persuasion

Norbert Aubuchon

AMACOM
American Management Association

New York • Atlanta • Boston • Chicago • Kansas City • San Francisco • Washington, D.C.
Brussels • Mexico City • Tokyo • Toronto

This book is available at a special
discount when ordered in bulk quantities.
For information, contact Special Sales Department,
AMACOM, a division of American Management Association,
1601 Broadway, New York, NY 10019.

This publication is designed to provide accurate and authoritative
information in regard to the subject matter covered. It is sold with the
understanding that the publisher is not engaged in rendering legal,
accounting, or other professional service. If legal advice or other expert
assistance is required, the services of a competent professional person
should be sought.

Library of Congress Cataloging-in-Publication Data

Aubuchon, Norbert.
    The anatomy of persuasion / Norbert Aubuchon.
        p.   cm.
    Includes bibliographical references and index.
    ISBN 0-8144-7952-9
        1. Negotiation in business.   2. Persuasion (Psychology)
3. Persuasion (Rhetoric)   4. Selling.   5. Leadership.
I. Title.
HD58.6.A93   1997
658.4'052—DC21   96–51050
                                                        CIP

The Anatomy of Persuasion® is a trademark of
Norbert Aubuchon, registered in the United States
Patent & Trademark Office.

© 1997 Norbert Aubuchon.
All rights reserved.
Printed in the United States of America.

This publication may not be reproduced,
stored in a retrieval system,
or transmitted in whole or in part,
in any form or by any means, electronic,
mechanical, photocopying, recording, or otherwise,
without the prior written permission of AMACOM,
a division of American Management Association,
1601 Broadway, New York, NY 10019.

Printing number

10   9   8   7   6   5   4   3   2

To the thousands of people who have participated or who will participate in our seminars. You are our invaluable source of inspiration and ideas.

Contents

Foreword

Who is he? I asked myself.

I was waiting to be served at a local store, as was my soon-to-be new friend. As I learned later, he was having similar thoughts about me. It wasn't long before we approached one another and introduced ourselves. It turned out that we looked familiar to each other because we had both been employed by the DuPont Company, although in different parts of the business.

The usual conversation between retirees began with the standard question about how we were keeping ourselves busy. Nib, Norbert's nickname, enthusiastically described the seminars he had been giving on the subject of persuasion. He had created, sold, given, and continued to give frequent seminars on the subject to the point where he could no longer handle by himself all the tasks necessary to running a successful training business.

While I had continued consulting and even dabbled in real estate and insurance sales, I jumped at the invitation from Nib to join him in presenting these seminars. We had both spent many years in marketing positions at DuPont and were quite familiar with persuasion techniques as they applied to selling ideas and products. Nib's concept fascinated me because he had taken a creative look at the broader aspects of persuasion as applied to the interactions of people in family, social, business, and other contexts of their lives. This went far beyond the narrow focus on persuasion's application to selling alone.

We were also familiar with the fact that some people with

excellent ideas seemed to have chronic difficulty in getting them accepted, whereas others, often with ideas of less merit, seemed to have little difficulty getting theirs accepted. Some people are intuitively better persuaders than others, but that doesn't help to recover the good ideas that founder because of the presenter's weak persuasion skills. Nib's idea is that persuasion is a logical, teachable process based on the specific mental process everyone uses when making a decision to buy, or not to buy, something, no matter what that something is.

Nib invited me to sit in on one of his seminars. The participants happened to be a group of DuPont engineers who had to sell their consulting services to businesses within DuPont against very capable outside competition. Although these engineers were recognized professional experts in their own technical fields, they were not as effective as they needed to be to sell themselves and their services within the company. They and I were impressed with the straightforward logic behind Nib's analytical approach to developing a persuasive message. I learned later that time after time Nib would receive calls from former seminar participants praising him for teaching them a technique that worked. And this is the unfailing truth of *The Anatomy of Persuasion*®.[1]

Now Nib has made the essential parts of the seminar available to a much wider audience through the publication of this easy-to-read book. Learning by reading requires an extra degree of self-discipline compared with learning through the interaction of people. A safe prediction is that a substantial majority of those who complete this book will rate the time spent one of the most profitable learning experiences of a lifetime.

I'm convinced that the ability to persuade people is one of the most important components of leadership. If your goal is to be more successful in any aspect of your life, then I urge you to learn and use the principles presented here. The rewards will be infinitely greater than the effort.

Leon F. Dumont
Kennett Square, Pennsylvania

---

1. *The Anatomy of Persuasion*® is a trademark registered in the United States Patent and Trademark Office.

Acknowledgments

The idea of this book seemed straightforward enough at first. It was to be a translation of my seminar-workshop to book form. This is the same seminar my colleagues and I have been giving successfully for over ten years. The seminar trainer's manual was fully scripted, so I believed the translation should go well. And it did go well—in principle.

Unfortunately, we were so accustomed to using the spoken word with live audiences that we were initially unprepared for the tighter discipline, the more precise demands of the written word. The translation turned out to be far from straightforward. Were it not for my associate, Leon F. Dumont, both the clarity and quality of this work as it stands would have been substantially less.

Lee, who agreed to be my working editor, was well-qualified for the task. Having presented *The Anatomy of Persuasion*® seminar-workshop many times, he knows the subject inside out. His years of management at the DuPont Company added a solid foundation for the judgment needed. Lee's patience, his professional skills and willingness to edit, to rewrite passages occasionally, to criticize thoughts, ideas, and word choices, like his other contributions, were invaluable. There are three more words that fit here—his *friendship* and *enthusiasm* and my *gratitude.*

There were others involved with the seminar itself:

Ian N. Hemming, also a retired DuPont executive, who undertook the job of marketing and selling the seminar. Ian made many suggestions as to content, drawing on his years in sales management at DuPont. He made substantial contributions in many ways.

Robert E. Kellar, who headed management training at ICI Americas, not only gave me an early start but also kept the seminar on as a regular part of the ICI training curriculum for many years.

Robert Heyburn, CEO of Compumark, who was not only my first, real paying customer but also my first repeat customer for the seminar.

Phillip L. Pennartz, who pioneered the use of *The Anatomy of Persuasion* as a management tool. Please see Chapter 19.

Marshall Newton, a friend at DuPont, who made a valuable suggestion that helped solve a basic marketing problem.

John F. Grove, president of York Graphic Services, who gets credit for the seed of the idea that eventually led to the seminar. John wanted to teach his people how to write single-page proposals that would digest the company's complex propositions and persuade readers to make buying decisions in principle without having to plow though the sheafs of detail involved in his business.

Participants, who are the thousands of nice people who have graced our seminar-workshops with their presence so far. We learned from each and hope they got as much or more from us.

Finally, there are friends who made many helpful suggestions.

The
Anatomy
of
Persuasion

Introduction

No matter where you are in life, whether young or old, no matter who you are, no matter what your occupation is, no matter what size your wallet is, no matter what your goals, hopes, or ambitions are, your ability to get others to do what you want them to do is the key to your success.

Persuasion as a *function* plays a dominant role in our interactions with others. Think of a typical day. How often are you in the position of persuading a family member, a friend, or a business associate to do something or not to do something? I'll wager a dozen times a day.

Now you do not need a seminar or a how-to book to teach you to be more persuasive when inviting someone to lunch. But think of the really important things you want—a new job, a new client, a promotion. Such things involve someone's cooperation, agreement, approval, investment, or support. Few of the really important things anyone accomplishes can be done in a vacuum.

In today's business and professional world, progress is wholly dependent on generating good ideas and then converting them to practice. It's ironic, but true, that we do not lack for good ideas. What is missing is our ability to gain the acceptance, approval, support, or encouragement of them from others.

Persuasion is a motivating form of communication in all walks of life. Sadly, most of us are not very good at it because we have not mastered the how-to *process* of persuasion. As a result, the world loses much of the ingenuity we have to offer. We are not as good as we need to be in convincing others of the value of our ideas. Not counting physical force, intimidation, manipulation, coercion, or extortion, there are only three methods anyone can use to get action from other people.

Can you name them?

If you cannot, take heart. Neither could the thousands of people we have asked over the many years of teaching the skill of persuasion. Most cannot name them offhand because they have not thought about their skills in getting action from other people.

Answer: *command, negotiate,* and *persuade.* These three methods are very different in nature. Each has its place.

- *Command* is used only when you are sure of your power and authority and only when neither of the other two methods has worked. Even in the military, ordering people to do things often has its disadvantages. It usually gains reluctant compliance at best. Command is usually a last resort and not infrequently used out of frustration or the inability to employ other methods.

- *Negotiation* is a powerful tool but has major limitations. Experienced people use it only when absolutely necessary. Even under the best of conditions, such as in so-called win-win situations, negotiation is fundamentally adversarial in nature. It's an eye for an eye and a tooth for a tooth. You give to get, or you don't get. For example, negotiation will work only when two conditions exist simultaneously: (1) when you have something to give up that the other side believes it must have, and (2) when the other side has something for which you are willing to trade. Otherwise, negotiation collapses. Mediation and arbitration can also form part of the negotiation process.

- *Persuasion* is usually the primary and preferred method of gaining desired action from others. It fits most situations better than the other two and does so with a positive psychology of interactive communications. It creates its own power position. Because its nature is nonadversarial, those persuaded almost always feel comfortable and satisfied with the outcome. Commanding people to do things or compromising them through negotiation often leaves ill feelings. Test this against your own experience. Haven't you felt more comfortable taking an action when it met your needs, when you made the decision without negotiated compromises, or, worse, being ordered to do it?

Persuasion is that quiet, unforced power that can move heaven and earth. It is the prime motivator of people. Mastery of its principles will give you a lifetime advantage. Knowledgeable people call it *leadership*! After all, what is more powerful than getting people to do what you want them to do and having them like it? Persuasion is a learnable skill. Without it, highly skilled people fail time after time when they should be succeeding time after time.

Able leaders believe that all three methods are important to meet the variety of demands placed upon them. They agree that the most valuable, the most useful, the most rewarding is persuasion. Thus, for people who want to learn motivation skills, the place to start is with persuasion—the powerhouse of the three motivational tools available to humankind. You can use it every day in every aspect of your life—personal, business, or professional. If you agree that the function of persuasion is important to you, you may also agree that mastering the how-to process of persuasion is also of equal importance.

The best way to develop persuasion skills is via a unique*, step-by-step, analytical thinking process that helps you to analyze, organize, and present information in a logical, persuasive manner. It works in any situation, with any idea, product, or service, whether tangible or intangible. It can be adapted to any mode of delivery, oral or written. Use of the principles, all of which you can learn here, will help you build a lifetime skill as a persuasive communicator. That will give you an important advantage in your ability to influence and motivate others to accept your proposals . . . buy your products . . . use your services . . . adopt your policies . . . hire you . . . promote you! The list is endless.

You can enhance your experience with this book by devel-

---

*Since 1982, my associates and I have consulted with hundreds of training and human resources managers who are exposed to the whole spectrum of available training. So far, all agree that the Anatomy of Persuasion is unique because of its step-by-step, analytical approach to the process of persuasion.

oping an actual proposal on a subject of your own choosing as you learn the principles. Note that for the purposes of this book, a proposal is any message, oral or written, intended to persuade someone to do something. A double benefit! You can produce something useful and learn a new skill at the same time. Specific guidance is given in Chapter 1. Meanwhile, start thinking of the most important persuasion tasks that you face right now.

As you focus on persuasion, keep two guidelines in mind. They are vital to your success:

1. *Believe that your ideas, products, or services must be sold.* Don't believe the old myth that if you build a better mousetrap, the world will beat a path to your door. That is just not so. Good ideas, above-average intelligence, and hard work are not enough. Many people with excellent, innovative ideas, products, and services have waited in vain for recognition and success to find them. Regrettably, the virtues of some of the best ideas are not self-evident to anyone other than their creators. The unvarnished truth is that very few things sell themselves. Therefore, moving ideas from concept to willing acceptance and use is a process. The process is called persuasion. The key words here are *willing acceptance,* because unless you persuade people, the best you can expect is compliance. Compliance is seldom good enough for long-term results.

2. *Believe that some ideas, products, or services are much more likely to succeed than others and that you can learn how to pick the likely winners in advance.* Imagine the power you gain with this advantage. Your success rate increases dramatically. Separating the winners from the losers takes some practice, but you can easily learn to do it. This skill is important because we all come up with poor ideas from time to time. It's inevitable. You have done it; I have done it. Worse, we will do it again. How many times have you awakened with a "great" new problem-solving idea only to find out in the harsh light of reality that your idea won't work? Unfortunately, these losers, being our own creations, often turn into lovable "pets." They charm us, destroy our perspective, and soak up huge chunks of valuable time.

The Anatomy of Persuasion, as a structured thinking process, will help you cut through to reality. You will know early on whether a given idea is likely to succeed or fail, and, more important, you will know *why.* You will reduce the many hours of unproductive thought and work devoted to these losers, thus avoiding much discouragement, dismay, and rejection.

How will you do this? You will learn to examine any idea realistically. Yes, I said *any* idea, be it your own or someone else's. You will learn how to escape your personal biases; you will come to reliable and reasoned decisions on the realistic value of ideas; you will know whether you should invest your time, effort, and/or your money. The result: You will devote yourself productively to the winners rather than wasting valuable time on the losers. Your success rate will improve dramatically.

If good ideas seem to be in short supply, it is partly because many excellent ideas, yours included, die silently in infancy. They never mature because they were not presented in an organized, concise, and persuasive manner so as to motivate people to accept and use them. Your enhanced ability to recognize good ideas and to win buy-in for them will put you miles ahead of other people. There is an important need here. Note what Jack Welch, CEO of General Electric, had to say on the subject: "In today's environment a corporation needs all the ideas it can get from its men and women." That is an observation good for all time.

The best results are possible through persuasion rather than negotiation. With negotiation the so called win-win outcomes are compromises at best. With persuasion you get buy-in with enthusiasm. Everyone leaves truly satisfied with needs and objectives met. This is not to say that negotiation techniques should not be used. Negotiation has its place, but in most situations you should try persuasion first.

The Anatomy of Persuasion, as a method of thinking, offers you two things:

1. *A personal tool,* something every individual can use as a lifetime discipline
2. *A management tool,* something that a group can use to

increase the flow of good ideas within an organization and suppress poor ideas that cannot work.

To many people this thinking process has become a way of life. They recognize that it will never become obsolete because the process we all use when we make a decision to buy (accept) or not to buy (reject) something will not change.

Among our "graduates" are many managers who have gone on to use *The Anatomy of Persuasion* as a powerful management tool. With our help as trainers, everyone in their groups or organizations has learned to use this structured, logical thinking technique. The result is fourfold: The flow of good ideas increases. The flow of poor ideas decreases. The process changes the culture when people and their efforts become integrated. The outcome is synergistic.

But you don't have to wait for your organization to develop persuasion skills as a group. You should move ahead to success on your own, because you can make a difference for yourself no matter what the rest of your world does.

That is the general idea, but let's be more specific about your individual needs regarding persuasion skill development. Before you move ahead, do some special thinking about yourself by answering two questions calculated to help people articulate their needs:

1. Why do you feel the need to improve your persuasion skills?
2. What kinds of problems have you had persuading people in the past?

After you have your preliminary ideas together, you will probably be interested to learn how others have answered the same questions.

How Others Have Answered the Questions:

Why Do You Feel the Need to Improve Your Persuasion Skills?

"I see other people gaining acceptance for their ideas, projects, and programs. Many times my ideas are better, but I don't get the results others get. I'd like to change that by becoming more persuasive."

"Motivating people is my prime need. As a manager, I want to learn how to stimulate the people who work for me, get them to be enthusiastic about their work, use their initiative rather than wait for me to tell them what to do."

"My job requires that I get cooperation from people in our company over whom I have no authority. I need to improve my persuasion skills to get that cooperation. My job depends on it."

"I am in sales. Competition is fierce. My job is not only to find new customers but, most important, to keep our present customers happy. Keeping our customers satisfied and away from competition is vital. Once lost, the cost in time, money, and effort to gain a customer back is much greater than keeping the customer in the first place. I need to get better at keeping customers."

"I am in engineering. We are constantly building, re-building, changing, modifying, adjusting. Each task usually requires approval from someone or another. My biggest frustration is getting the approvals. I often spend more time doing that than I do solving problems. I need to learn how to get buy-in faster without wasting time hashing over details."

"I am in management information systems (MIS). New, complex computer technology (both hardware and software) forces change on us almost faster than we can comprehend it. Persuading people in our organization to understand and accept and adopt new computerized programs is a real task. I am not as good at it as I need to be."

"As a director-level manager, my job is to communicate with top management. I have to deal with our president and CEO almost every day. But there are five other directors competing for their attention and approval. My task is to get in there with better ideas, present them more persuasively, get approval, and get out without a lot of folderol. I don't do this as well as two of the other directors. I need to improve."

"My job involves total quality management (TQM). This means continuous quality improvement. And this means we must maintain a constant stream of good, usable ideas. We must get these ideas accepted and put to use. The problem is getting buy-in for these new ideas. People resist change. Change is the name of the game. I need to do two things: (1) get a better way to separate the good ideas from the bad ones before I try to sell them, and (2) find a way to sell these good, new ideas better and faster to carry out the continuous improvement process. Even continuous improvement needs continuous improvement."

"I used to be in field sales, where I did an outstanding job. I was good enough to be promoted to national sales manager. Now, instead of selling products to customers, I have to sell ideas to management. This is very different, because every idea is different. One day I'm asking for price changes; another day I'm asking for changes in the distribution system; then it's about compensation or computers or company cars. Internal selling is more difficult because it involves more written proposals to back up group presentations. I need to improve my ability to collect new information, analyze it, organize it, and present it concisely—both written and oral."

"I am in research and development. My job is to come up with ideas to improve current products and processes and to create new ones. The people who work with me are very creative; we have a flow of good ideas, but only a few get accepted. Example, a competitor recently introduced a product we developed five years ago and couldn't "sell" to management. My persuasion skills need serious improvement. Too much good stuff is falling through the 'cracks.' "

What Kinds of Problems Have You Had Persuading People in the Past?

"Getting my thoughts organized properly. I'm really not sure exactly what information should be presented first and why; what should come next and why; what should come after that and so on. Sometimes I do this right and get acceptance, but too often I don't get acceptance."

"When I fail to get acceptance with what I think is a perfectly acceptable idea, I don't know what was really wrong with the proposal. I guess I don't understand the persuasion process. I know I am missing something, because I see other people hit their targets much more often than I do. I need help and hope you can give it."

"Even when I present an idea in a face-to-face conversation, my management often asks me to put it in writing. They want a one-or two-page memo and not a full report. 'Just give me the facts,' my boss says. I find this difficult, because I have trouble boiling my ideas down to short, readable, persuasive messages that get approval. I wind up writing and writing and writing. I need to learn how to bring order out of the chaos I create with thousands of words."

"I want to find a way to develop proposals faster and get more consistent results. I do good work on this sometimes, but not always. I need a system that will improve my ability to think through and develop consistently good persuasive messages."

"Executive summaries bug me. These are the one-page cover letters on our proposals. The executive summary is very important. It is supposed to tell the decision maker all he/she needs to know to make a decision in principle without reading the ponderous material attached. When we do the executive summary right, we usually get the business. And when we don't, we don't. Unfortunately, we are not consistent. We need to improve our persuasion skills so we can do this right every time. Our proposals are big, thick things with lots of details—too much to wade through. We have to do it this way because we sell complex, high-cost products. It has to be complete and, above all, persuasive."

If *your* answers to the two questions tell you that you really need to gain a peak performance level in persuading people to act on your ideas, accept your proposals, buy your products, use your services, adopt your policies, hire you, retain you, promote you, elect you, or appoint you, then stick with this book. You will gain a lifetime skill that works. These are the pluses:

- Your success rate in winning acceptance for your ideas and motivating people will increase dramatically.
- You will learn how to prepare written proposals in an easy-to-read, single-page format that will get action.
- Your oral proposals and presentations will be more effective.
- You will, with practice, become an expert in persuasion.
- You will gain a reputation as a clear thinker.
- You will master the art of brevity in your communications.
- Your persuasion skills will make you a more effective force in the workplace and elsewhere because you will be able to make more things happen.
- You will use these same persuasion skills in every part of your life from now on: in your business or professional life and with family and friends.
- You will learn and apply two important principles of communication that very few people know about or understand.
- You will be able to pick winning ideas and avoid the losers. You will be able to predict which ideas, products, and services are likely to get buy-in and which won't.
- You will learn to identify the "hot buttons" in people, because you will know how to focus on, listen for, remember, and analyze their needs.
- You will think, talk, and write in terms of *benefits* that everybody wants instead of *things* that nobody wants.
- To repeat, the word for this is *leadership*!

More specifically, here is what each chapter of this book offers you.

Chapter 1: Overview

This chapter opens by positioning the importance of persuasion as a personal skill. Then it summarizes what the book is about, namely the two interactive thinking processes involved in persuasion. The first thinking process is the one we all use when we make a decision to buy or not to buy anything. The second thinking process helps you get the specific action you want from others. You also will learn exactly how to enhance your experience with this book by developing a winning proposal of your own as you go along. The Preparation Guidelines presented here will help you get started.

Chapter 2: Creativity

A key element in developing persuasion skill is the ability to think creatively. Persuaders must collect diverse information and then turn it into ideas that match opportunity. They must stimulate minds, solve problems, create improvements, transform apathy to enthusiasm, and gain acceptance. This chapter offers some useful suggestions on how to enhance your own creative power.

Chapter 3: Two Principles of Communication

Two important and often overlooked principles of communication are described here. The first principle will help you fix responsibility for all communications. If you accept it as doctrine, it will put you in charge of your own communications and help you pinpoint responsibility for those of others. The second principle explains the vital importance of learning how to structure messages so that they mesh and interact with the thinking processes, or mind-sets, of the people you want to reach.

Chapter 4: The Buying Process

This chapter introduces the first of the two thinking processes. As you examine this five-step decision-making process, you will become consciously aware that this is the process you use when you make your buying decisions. It is the very same process that you must influence in others when trying to persuade them to "buy" your idea.

Chapter 5: The Persuasion Process: Part I

This is the second of the two thinking processes and, like the first, it also has five steps. It is the foundation of the persuasion skill you can use for the rest of your life. You will learn how the process works in principle and see an actual proposal created using the process.

Chapter 6: Needs

Of the five steps in the persuasion process, the most important concerns needs. Your ability to discover and interpret the needs of others is essential to your success. The study of needs is just as complex as is the study of human behavior because human needs are the motivators of human behavior. This chapter defines the two major categories of needs and shows you how they interact.

Chapter 7: The Persuasion Process: Part II

This chapter elaborates on the five steps of the persuasion process as you will be using it. It builds on the two basic processes, buying and persuasion, and the principles that govern them.

Chapter 8: Controlling the Persuasion Process

The five steps of the persuasion process are not quite enough by themselves. You will need certain controls to help keep your logic in focus and your thinking effective. The three controls presented here will aid your development of a persuasive argument by keeping it on track.

Chapter 9: Features, Functions, and Benefits

Your ability to translate a feature (a thing) into a benefit (what the thing does) is an indispensable skill in the art of persuasion. People are interested in what things can do for them. You will become an expert translator of features to benefits, and you will know where functions fit in the scheme once you have read this chapter.

Chapter 10: Setting Your Objective

A key element in the development of a successful proposal is its objective. Your ability to set clear, concise, unambiguous objectives for your proposals is essential. The objective for any proposal will influence all the other parts. The suggestions in this chapter will help you to keep your proposals on target.

Chapter 11: Using the Tools

All the pieces will come together for you in this chapter. You will see a complete, successful proposal done in the most effective style. The writer, using one page only, proposes to a prospective buyer of an old, rundown apartment building that he hire her to coordinate a rehabilitation project from start to finish. You will identify the parts of her proposal and see the structure. You will also see how this person constructed her proposal using the Outline Guide, a short form complete with easy-to-read instructions to help you prepare your own proposals.

Chapter 12: Case Study: How to Increase a Staff During a Hiring Freeze

Now you can try your hand at preparing a proposal using given information. You are a marketing executive trying to persuade your boss to let you employ someone when the company is restricting new hires. You will use the Outline Guide again to help you with a somewhat more complicated task. A sample answer sheet will give you extra guidance.

Chapter 13: Case Study: How to Get Funding for Your Program

Here is another chance for you to develop a proposal using the Outline Guide. This time you are a production manager in a large plant, that is in the midst of an expansion needed to meet increasing demand. A sudden and unexpected business downturn develops. Your boss tells you to end the expansion project immediately without further expense. Realizing that spending a little more money now to tie up loose ends will save money in the long run, you want to change his mind.

Chapter 14: Case Study: How to Be a Rocket Scientist!

Let's try one more proposal. You have become a rocket scientist. Your task is to convince your boss to let you change the research direction at a critical time in an important project. All the information is provided for you to shape a proposal that should sway the boss to your way of thinking. The Outline Guide will escort you through this exercise, and a sample answer sheet will give you extra guidance.

Chapter 15: Building Your Own Proposal

By now you will be ready to put your new skills to work on something real. You can start building your own proposal on a subject important to you, using all the principles discussed in this book. With the Preparation Guidelines, develop your information and apply it to the Outline Guide. From that you will come out with a proposal in outline form.

All you will then need to do is flesh out your work to suit whatever mode of delivery you have chosen—a group presentation, a face-to-face situation, a concise, single-page memo, a letter, an advertisement, or any other format. Result: With this effort, you will have developed a real proposal to get the action you want.

Chapter 16: A Touch of the Real World

Just as we absorb the basics of something new, just as we become skilled enough to enjoy our accomplishment and dare to venture forth, we are promptly disabused by practical experience. We rise from rookie to professional competence by learning to cope with reality. Forewarning can lessen the impact of the inevitable nasty surprises. This chapter offers samples of the kinds of situations you may face and some helpful advice learned the hard way.

Chapter 17: Can You Find the Errors?

By the time you get this far, you will have developed skill at the persuasion process. A little practice is in order. Imagine that you are in one of our seminar-workshops. The other participants, having prepared actual proposals, are about to present their work to the group for analysis and constructive criticism. Your task is to study each proposal, identify any errors, and suggest specific corrections. Three proposals are presented for your appraisal.

Chapter 18: Selling Your Ideas to Higher Management

Most people who are part of an organization will tell you that one of their most difficult tasks is getting acceptance for their ideas from higher management. Even professional salespeople, those trained to sell products or services to outside customers, agree that selling their own ideas within their organizations usually is harder than their regular selling work. There is one clear observation, however. While "internal selling" is difficult for most people, an anointed few breeze through and get acceptance time after time. Why?

Chapter 19: *The Anatomy of Persuasion* as a Management Tool

This chapter will describe how you as a manager can use these principles as a tool to improve the flow of good ideas within your organization and, at the same time, reduce the flow of poor ideas. This can be a boon to any manager interested in using group synergism to meet the rapidly changing conditions of our times. A case history and a recipe are here to guide your progress.

A Final Word: Thinking and Talking in Terms of Benefits

Benefits! That's what people buy. But a benefit to one person may not appeal to another. As you know, finding the operative benefit in any situation is the key to successful persuasion and personal satisfaction. This chapter is a final reminder of an easy way to think and talk in terms of benefits. And it defines your path to success in terms of benefits.

Four separate appendixes offer A Checklist of Common Errors, Preparation Guidelines, an Outline Guide, and a Structure and Alignment Chart.

1

Overview

Arthur "Red" Harrison Motley, the former chairman of *Parade* magazine, expressed the vital importance of persuasion in one short sentence: *"Nothing happens until someone sells something."* Red Motley's second career was preaching the importance of persuasion as a personal skill. He knew that persuasion is the fuel of all human activity. He knew it as the leadership force that anyone can apply to make things happen. Red Motley did much more than carry the message. He proved the power of persuasion personally through his leadership. He moved *Parade* from a small venture to a publishing giant with a weekly circulation of 20 million copies. It now sells more than 37 million copies weekly. *Parade* magazine is a monument to Motley's personal success and an example for those who wish to make things happen.

As a case in point, imagine that we are in a blimp looking down on a factory in the middle of a field. You can see raw materials going in. Someone has sold someone there on buying those specific materials. You see the finished products coming out and shipped away. Obviously, someone has sold that output to users. Someone is selling the people who work on working there. And what about the beginnings of the enterprise? Someone persuaded someone else to invest money and build the factory in the first place. Persuasion is a key element in the success of this activity.

The "nothing happens until someone sells something" is the reason persuasion as a force is needed more today than ever before. Revolutions are occurring everywhere. Words like *down-sizing* and *reengineering* characterize some of these huge, ongoing changes. Job security as we once knew it is gone. People recognize the importance of building personal skills to meet rapidly changing demands. Business and professional cultures are embracing continuous improvement in one form or another. Continuous improvement demands ongoing creation and the adoption of new ideas. Thus, change is central to all such efforts. Change per se is a process, and the ability to make change happen is a skill.

Change is seldom spontaneous. When you see an organization in which changes are occurring regularly and without serious disorder, you can bet there are people somewhere in that organization who are skilled persuaders. They make change happen with alacrity. Quality programs, corporate reengineering, and other efforts that require change will not work very well—or at all—in organizations that lack such people.

The presence of a problem is often the absence of an idea. If you can generate good ideas to solve problems or to create improvements, take your next step. Become skilled at winning acceptance for your ideas from the people who have the power to put them to use. With that will come a bonus benefit. Your persuasion skills will put you in a leadership position vis-à-vis people who have good ideas but do not know how to get buy-in for them. Such people will come to you. Remember, there is no shortage of ideas, only a shortage of competent advocates.

This book is about *thinking processes*. Two interactive thinking processes are involved. The *first* thinking process is the one we all use when we make a decision to buy or not to buy anything. Whenever we consider buying anything, whether it is an idea or something tangible, we all use the same decision-making process. Most of us are not consciously aware of this mental mechanism. Gaining awareness of this buying process in yourself is important because it is this very same process in others that you must influence in order to win acceptance for your proposals.

The *second* thinking process helps you to get the specific action you want. It shows you how to influence the buying process in others. These two processes mesh and interact. The first process, your target, tells you what you need to do; the second process tells you how to do it.

This book is not about delivery skills such as writing, public speaking, discussion leading, presenting, or showmanship. These come later. Your first task is to think through and develop structure and content in your messages. Only after thoughtful preparation does the method of delivery become an issue. The intent here is not to minimize the importance of delivery skills. It is simply to put first things first.

You can enhance your experience with this book by developing a proposal of your own as you go along. This way you will do something productive while you learn. Your new skill will start serving you immediately. Begin by choosing a subject on which to develop your proposal and then following the guidelines given:

Preparation Guidelines

- Select a business or professional subject that is important to you personally.
- Pick a subject that is both important and timely, one that can be acted on soon.
- Define your objective in a clear, concise manner, and write it out in fifty words or less. This is your message to yourself. It should state exactly what you want to accomplish with this persuasion task. It is for your eyes only.
- Identify the needs of the person(s) you wish to persuade. Be sure those needs reflect that person's views, not your own. (Your needs should be defined in your fifty-word objective statement.)
- Quantify important elements of your proposal, for example, costs, time, number of people required, quality, quantity or performance numbers, earnings and pay back. . . .

You do not need to prepare a formal, finished proposal. The main thing is to be well-informed on the subject you have chosen.

2

Creativity

A key element in developing persuasion skill is the ability to think creatively. Persuaders must collect diverse information and assemble it into ideas that match opportunity. They must stimulate minds, solve problems, create improvement, transform apathy into enthusiasm, and gain acceptance. Persuasion deals with the future, because it focuses on what could be.

Characteristics of Creativity

A better understanding of your creative thinking process will enhance your powers of persuasion. This chapter is not a treatise on creativity as a whole; instead it provides a few useful insights into how your creativity works plus some tips on how you can manage it more effectively. Four important characteristics of the creative process deserve your special attention: *objective, input, processing,* and *output.* With these in mind, you can stimulate and guide your creative process more effectively.

Creativity is your business. There is no inner sanctum that admits only creative types such as artists, writers, actors, musicians, inventors, and scientists. Nor is it the private domain of psychologists and psychiatrists. We can learn a lot from all these people, but creativity is an individual property. Yours is yours. Mine is mine. What each of us does with it is up to us.

Output

Let's start by thinking first about the end of the creative process, the *output.* This is the arrival of an idea, that gratifying experience we wait for when we are seeking a new idea. It's the result, that magic, luminous moment when an idea pops into our awareness. It's an event! A breakthrough! At these times we experience strong feelings, such as joy, excitement, and elation. Were you to describe such a moment, you might mention a source of sudden illumination such as a bolt of lightning or a light bulb turning on. You probably have said, "This morning, it finally dawned on me that . . ." or "It came to me in a flash." Almost everyone characterizes this invisible event—an idea popping into one's conscious mind from one's "unconscious" mind*—in terms of a visible, sudden happening. It is an unmistakable revelation that lets us "see" everything. Some scientists use the word *elegant* when they describe something pristine, pure, and uncorrupted such as a fresh, new idea.

This output represents the remarkable working relationship between our two minds, the unconscious and the conscious. Together they form a marvelous mechanism with a dynamic balance. This gives us a process that collects information and then digests, manipulates, juggles, modifies, cuts, reshapes, rearranges, assembles, and finally puts forth ideas.

Rollo May, psychiatrist and author of the best-selling book *The Courage to Create,* wrote of Carl Jung's idea of our two minds: "Jung often made the point that there is polarity, a kind of opposition between the unconscious experience and the conscious. He believed the relationship was (is) compensatory: consciousness controls the wild, illogical vagaries of the unconscious, while the unconscious keeps consciousness from drying up in banal, empty, arid rationality." May also observed that our unconscious, with all its wildness, seems to have fun with our more serious conscious mind by breaking up our most rigid thinking with radical notions.† Perhaps this is why many highly creative adults exhibit such refreshing, youthful qualities.

This process of forming and building ideas goes on in the unconscious mind, though we are not aware of it. The philosopher William James once said that we learn to swim in the winter and to ice skate in the summer. He was speaking of

---

Unconscious is used here as a catchall term for the subconscious, preconscious, and other dimensions of the mind below full awareness.
†Rollo May, *The Courage to Create* (New York: Norton, 1975), p. 59.

neurological processes that continue even when we are not working on them. While we cannot actually control these processes, we can influence them through random input such as thinking about ice skating in the summer.

I recall an experience of this kind. In the earliest stage of my training as a Naval Aviator, I was having trouble with the three-dimensional control system of the airplane. My coordination of hands, feet, eyes, and seat of the pants just did not work well enough. My instructor told me to get a stick about three feet long to represent the joy stick (the main control device in the airplane). He told me to go to the barracks, sit on my bunk, put one end of the stick on the floor and make believe I was using it in flying a plane. He told me to push the stick back and forth gently and imagine the nose going up and down. He said to move the stick sideways and involve my feet on make-believe rudder pedals. I was to make turns, dives, and climbs. "Get it deep in your mind," he said. After several sessions, I returned to the airplane to discover that I had learned to fly in the barracks. I was amazed. My instructor was not. He was no psychologist, but he knew how to put my unconscious to work productively.

Does this suggest that we can consciously influence the "wild, illogical vagaries of the unconscious" to get an output of useful ideas? Will it help with persuasion? The answer is yes. To explain how, let's examine other characteristics of the creative process.

Objective

Conventional wisdom has it that if you have a clear objective before you start your creative process, you are more likely to achieve your goal. A story about Archimedes (287?–212 B.C.), the famous Greek scientist, is a case in point. Archimedes was the science guru in King Hiero's court at Syracuse. The king had bought a new crown from the local goldsmith. He was delighted with it. The design and artistic detail were superb. The crown fit comfortably. There was, however, one nagging question. The king was concerned that the goldsmith might have ripped him off by diluting the gold with a cheaper metal, and he asked Archimedes to figure out if the goldsmith had cheated him.

As Archimedes examined the crown, he pulled out his knife to take a small sample of the metal from the crown for assay purposes. The king stopped him, saying that the crown was not to be damaged even in a small way. He ordered Archimedes to find other means of answering the question. Archimedes pondered for days trying to think of a solution to the king's question. One day, while taking his bath, he noticed that his body displaced the water as it entered the tub. Previously, this had been an irrelevant observation. This time, however, it took on special meaning.

"Eureka!" he shouted, as an idea popped into his mind. Suddenly he knew exactly how to measure the gold content in the crown. The idea was clear, complete, and elegant. Archimedes ran to the king with the news. Think about this situation. Think of the many baths Archimedes must have taken without making a connection between the displacement of water and anything else, let alone the king's problem. Even more important, he discovered a far-reaching principle: how to measure the volume of an irregularly shaped object.

Nothing happens in a vacuum. Archimedes had no reason to think about either the problem or the solution until he had developed an objective. The king's request did that for him. The objective started the problem-solving process and guided the creative effort efficiently. By now Archimedes knew what he was about and where he was trying to go.

An objective is the foundation of efficient, effective creative thinking. Archimedes' objective caused him to make new connections from old observations. Water displacement, irrelevant before, now became important under the conditions created by the objective. Bingo! Well-thought-out objectives will help you govern and guide all your thinking processes. Without them you will be at the mercy of chance, luck, and serendipity.

Input

Your creative power also depends on the supply of data stored in your mind. The output is not haphazard. It relates to what you have collected through observation, investigation, listening, discussion, reading, or doing. Some people doubt this, believing they have produced ideas "out of the blue." A thorough search of the memory usually reveals the connection.

Your objective usually influences what you notice, absorb, and connect. If you are thinking about combustion, you are not likely to notice much about horticulture. Keeping your objective in focus helps you exert control over your creative process. Balance is necessary to keeping an open mind. If your data gathering is limited, you may miss a key element. Here is a case in point.

Processing

Another characteristic of the arrival of the idea is the timing or circumstances associated with the event. You may have noticed that your ideas usually arrive at a certain time of the day or under particular circumstances. Some people say that they get their ideas when they are taking a shower, while eating breakfast, driving to or from work, in the middle of the night, and so on. Others say that their ideas arrive under certain circumstances—after a period of diversion or relaxation, for example.

Perhaps you have noticed a similar pattern in yourself. You have been concentrating for hours, working hard on a project. You are trying to develop something brand-new or maybe just trying to solve a difficult problem. You have been gathering information. Finally you are saturated. You are tired, fed up, frustrated, feeling stressed and depressed. You just cannot pull all the pieces together. At this stage, you wonder why your good common sense ever allowed you to get into such a project to begin with. Your fatigue, frustration, and desperation tell you to relax and turn to something completely different for a while. You may read, watch TV, play tennis or golf, eat or sleep. As you suspend work, you leave the task to natural mental digestive processes. Your unconscious quietly goes to work processing the data.

Then, in due course, an idea pops out of your unconscious and into your conscious mind. Your "light bulb" goes on! The idea arrives, and you work with it with the same intensity you applied before. Unless you end the matter by turning to another subject, you may continue with other creative cycles and more outputs to enhance your project.

Creative cycles are predictable. Think of your own pattern and then adapt to it. The purpose of the overnight assignment in our seminar-workshops is just this. Most people produce ideas after strenuous input followed by rest. People connect their own ideas with the new information and develop remarkably good proposals the first time around. This is why we suggest you create your own proposal as you learn the principles presented in this book.

The Recipe

By way of summary, bear in mind that creativity is a process. It's yours. Start it with an *objective* to control the general direction. Undertake intensive *input* to the point of fatigue. Divert yourself to rest and relaxation to let the *processing* happen; *output* will follow. If by chance an idea does not appear, most likely your unconscious does not have enough material to work on. Repeat the input-diversion cycles again and again. You will produce usable ideas and dramatically improve your power of persuasion.

3

Two Principles of Communication

To be effective as a persuader, you must become a good communicator. To do that you must apply two often ignored principles of communication. These are worthy of your special attention because they are universal. You can apply them to all your communications, whatever their purpose.

Principle 1: Taking Responsibility

When you are the sender of a communication, you must take 100 percent of the responsibility for the creation, transmission, and delivery of the message.

This means that you, as the sender, relieve your intended receiver of all responsibility. In other words, it is your job to get your message to its destination and get it across, that is, understood. In turn, when your intended receiver responds, the full responsibility falls on that person for his or her message. Having switched to the role of receiver, you then have no responsibility. Thus, this first principle keeps both the responsibility and the authority in the same place, always with the sender.

To examine this further, let's divide communication functions into the sender's part and the receiver's part. The message is the sender's idea. The sender wants to tell someone something. The sender creates the message, selects the receiver, arranges the mode of delivery, and sends the message. Suppose the message gets there, but the receiver does not understand it or, worse, misunderstands it. Either way, the intended message was not received. The failure, obviously, was with the sender—no one else.

Think of a dialogue. As each person speaks and becomes the sender, the responsibility switches. Even when the receiver is eagerly waiting for the message, it is still the sender's responsibility to do what is necessary to get the message to the receiver and understood. If you do not accept the responsibility and act appropriately when you are the sender, communication failure is certain. This shortfall happens frequently. I'm sure you have heard (or even participated in) a two-way communication failure like this ridiculous, but common, bit of dialogue:

"Look at what you've done. You've locked us out *again*. I told you to bring the keys. How are we going to get this door unlocked?"

"What do you mean, *again*?"

"You do this all the time. You don't listen. You're off in some other world. . . ."

"I thought *you* had the keys."

"I distinctly told *you* to bring the keys. But you didn't listen. You never listen. . . ."

"*You* were last out of the house. Why didn't you check?"

"Because I told *you* to bring the keys."

"I didn't hear you, *obviously*."

"You are supposed to be listening, *obviously*."

"How can I listen when I can't hear you?"

"Maybe you need a hearing aid."

"You're supposed to listen too."

"What are you mumbling about now?"

"You're the one who needs a hearing aid."

"Stop mumbling and figure out how to get this damn door unlocked. . . . "

As the sender, it is my job to know what you, the receiver, can and cannot understand and then to act accordingly. Suppose we have a French-English language barrier. As sender, I must get the message translated so that you can understand it. Obviously, you are not waiting breathlessly to hear from me. You may not even know or care who I am.

Those who ignore the first principle (You must take 100 percent of the responsibility for the creation and delivery of the message) do so at their own peril. But, by taking the responsibility, you gain control of the only part of the communications process you can hope to control, namely your own part. Explore and test this principle further. You may find some gray areas or even some obscure exceptions. But, in the end, you will decide your acceptance of full responsibility as a communicator is critical to your success.

Accepting responsibility is one thing; doing something about it is another. Preparing a message so that your receiver can understand it is usually far more complicated than translating a message from one language to another. Your message must be compatible with the knowledge and background of your receiver. If you are a lawyer sending a technical message about criminal law to an engineer or a physician, you should express the matter in lay terms. This should go without saying. Unfortunately, it is often necessary to spell it out.

Nearly everyone unintentionally fogs messages by not considering the knowledge and background of the intended receiver. Perhaps we just do not spend enough time thinking about the other person's frame of mind. Some people, in fact most of us at one time or another, take fanciful ego trips by using exotic or unusual words that are beyond the pale for others. Sometimes we use verbal shorthand, forgetting that our intended receiver may not be privy to our jargon. Technical, specialized, scientific, legal, accounting, medical, or engineering terms and expressions will fit perfectly for some messages but destroy others, depending on the receiver.

When in doubt, test. Years ago I worked with a physicist who specialized in radiation and radiographic imaging. He was a great communicator because he recognized the vital importance of expressing technical information accurately in lay terms. Like others who have been successful at this, he also appreciated the difficulty of such tasks. When working together on a piece of writing of this sort, he and I were frequently dismayed by our test results. We often discovered that our "clear, lucid, expressive language" failed miserably when reviewed by the people we used to simulate our intended receivers. We went back to rewriting often. Such advance testing avoided serious communication failures. The stakes, incidentally, were high; we were dealing with medical procedures involving the treatment of cancer. Whatever you do, a good rule is to use short sentences built out of short, commonly used words whenever you can.

Principle 2: Interacting With the Receiver

The sender must structure messages so that they mesh and interact with the thinking process of the receiver.

In other words, if you do not structure your messages properly, they are not likely to be received as you intended them to be, and the responses may be unsatisfactory. Conversely, properly structured messages "turn on" and influence the thinking processes of your target audience; they feed data suitable to the mind-set of your receiver. Thus, the information you send is in the proper shape and does not need further processing to be easily understood.

If you can learn the mental process a person uses for a given action, you have a much better chance of influencing the behavior of that person. This is not as difficult as it may sound, because there are many mental processes common to all of us. We all use the same kind of computer—our brains. We all use essentially the same structured processes for the same kinds of functions.

Think of our structuring behavior in concrete terms. When we build a bridge, we use a design that functions well for the purpose, such as a cantilever, arch, or suspension device. When we want to float something, we build a hull; we construct an airframe for flying, and a wheel for rolling. Structure governs the creation of operas, plays, music, poetry, novels, articles, scholarly papers, and so on. The fundamentals of these structures remain constant through the ages because they work. Reinvention usually is both unnecessary and unwise.

Now think of our structuring behavior in abstract terms. Think of your own mind, how it structures the information it must deal with in specific situations. You are going grocery shopping. You probably have a mental checklist—some way to collect the needed information about variables such as weather, what to wear, and what to buy. You probably have developed a routine for closing windows, locking doors, and caring for a cat or dog. You think about exactly where you will go, the route to take, the timing, the money you will need, the credit cards, car keys, the car itself, and so on. You have done this so often that you have become structured to the task. You have found a way to do something that works for you. It is a timesaving tool. With it you do not need to rethink the task every time. Another benefit is that you do not have to correct mistakes because you do not make them. You always have your driver's license, your money, a list of things to buy and do. It works.

If you dig deeper into your own structuring processes, you may find that you have a prescribed order for accumulating information. There is an order to your thinking—first things first, second things second, and so on. These priorities are based on reasoning that makes sense to you. For example, when planning that trip to the grocery store, you decide what you want to buy before you decide when to go or what to wear.

Thus, as we think about the task of creating messages to mesh with the thinking process of the receiver, we also need to think about what that person is trying to do. Then we need to learn how he or she thinks through the task. What are the priorities, the logic, the flow? Once we know these things, we can decide how to influence that process with a structured message that will mesh and interact effectively.

To keep this idea simple and workable, let's focus on a real example. Imagine yourself as a manager in a certain large consumer-products company. You have learned to use a special structure in memos to convey information about the business to other managers in your company because it matches the way everyone there thinks about the management of the business. The most significant information, the conclusion or the central idea, is presented first. This is followed by supporting data presented in a prescribed manner, according to the information's decreasing order of importance. It is called the inverted-pyramid structure.

The inverted pyramid works well for you and others for two reasons. First, readers need to know the writer's central idea before they can appreciate the relevance of the other information in the memo. Second, when readers read a memo, they are in a hurry to stop reading. They are busy. They seek only the information they need at the time without having to sort through extraneous data. This structure, familiar to readers in your company, permits effective communication to happen quickly and efficiently.

An analogy is a kitchen structure. When you are in your own, you are comfortable because you know where things are. You can produce a simple breakfast of coffee, toast, and cereal quickly. You have perfected a routine. But if you must make the same breakfast in my kitchen, you will need more time to find what you need because my system is different. Think of how much slower the process would be if you were forced to make your breakfast in a different kitchen every morning unless, of course, all kitchens were set up exactly as your own at home.

All the people working in your company use the same kind of "kitchen." They all structure their communications by using the established inverted-pyramid thinking process. Thus they get desired results rapidly and effectively. And the business runs efficiently. Other people in different organizations may require information organized in different ways for different purposes. In summary, structuring is the simple matter of putting things in the right places.

To apply the second principle to the persuasion task, we must understand the thinking process we all use when we decide whether to buy something. This thinking process will be covered in Chapter 4. You need to know how it works because this "buying process" is the key to your persuasion skill. In short, you must structure your persuasive messages to mesh and interact with the thinking process of the person to be persuaded.

Whenever the subject of communications is discussed, brevity often is a central issue. Unfortunately, the virtues of brevity are often misunderstood. Brevity isn't of value by itself. Just because a message is brief, it is not necessarily a concise, effective communication. Therefore, seeking brevity for its own sake is likely to be ruinous.

You can put brevity in its proper place by remembering the definition of good design. This says that form follows function. This also defines good communications. Brevity is form but not function. Structure provides function but not form. Simply squeezing everything onto one page will not do. You must build structure first. Get the structure right, and the rest will usually take care of itself, just as form follows function in anything that is of good design.

In summary, the first principle says that when you are the sender of a communication, you must take 100 percent responsibility for the creation, transmission, and intelligibility of the message. The second principle says that the sender must structure messages so that they mesh with the thinking process of the receiver.

4

The Buying Process

This chapter introduces the first of the two thinking processes in *The Anatomy of Persuasion*. As you examine this five-step decision-making process, you will become consciously aware that this is the process you use when you make your buying decisions. Then you will know without doubt that when you wish to be persuasive, this is the very same process you must influence in others.

You will recall that in Chapter 3 we identified two often ignored principles of good communication. The second principle was that the *sender must structure messages to mesh and interact with the thinking process of the receiver.* If you can learn the thinking processes a person uses for a given action and find ways to address these processes, you will have a much better chance of influencing the behavior of that person. You will know not only the kinds of information that person is seeking but also how the information will be processed and used. This requirement may seem daunting at first because there are thousands, maybe millions, of thinking processes that people use for different purposes.

An excellent way to learn the structured thinking process of another person is to examine something that that person did, then find out *how* it was done. What was the objective, the rationale, the steps, and the conclusion? Now compare that process with the one you would use for the same task. By now you should be close enough to define the process. If in doubt, reconfirm your conclusions. Ask friends how they think through the same exercise. This will work out well because we all use essentially the same structured processes for the same kinds of functions. To process our information, we all use the same kind of "computer"—our brains.

For a practical application, think about your own behavior when you decide to buy a car. You have been through this often, yet you may not be fully conscious of the process you use any more than you are conscious of the process you use to control the muscle groups that move your legs and keep you in balance when you walk.

Please remember, we are dealing with *one thinking process.* No matter what you are considering (whether it is intangible or tangible, inexpensive or costly, personal or impersonal), the decision-making process is the same. Thousands of people in our seminar-workshops have examined these steps critically, and more than 99 percent have agreed that this is the five-step thinking process they use to arrive at a buying decision. Therefore, we can vouch for its reliability with confidence. You can cast this concept in stone and depend on it along with the law of gravity.

The Five Orderly Parts to Our Buying Process

Needs

Your buying process begins when you have an unsatisfied need. None of us does anything without a need. It supplies our motivation. This is not a need that someone else says you have or ought to have. It is your need as you see it, know it, or feel it. Such a need may be in the forefront of your mind or it may be obscure. Your need might be real or imagined, concrete or abstract, rational or irrational; but your need must be there in some form.

Recognition

The mere presence of a need is not enough to stimulate action. You must recognize the need as being sufficiently important, in comparison to all others, for you to rate it as a top priority and worthy of your immediate attention and action. Once you have done so, you have completed the first two steps in the buying process: You have a *need,* and you have *recognized* it as something you want to fill. You move to your next step.

Search

Now you are in the active part of the buying mode. You are in search of ways to fill your recognized need. You are on a "shopping" trip. This might involve a quick and easy search, as in buying a candy bar. Or it might be an arduous, protracted task, as in buying a house. No matter what you are seeking, you continue your search until you feel you have collected enough information on which to base a final decision.

Evaluation

You study and digest what you collected during your search. By some process of your own, you match your findings against your need requirements. You develop various options and choices. Your evaluation includes some sort of rating system, simple or complex, depending on your project.

Decision

Finally, with your information in suitable order, you make a decision. It may be to take a specific action on the basis of positive data. Or you may decide against taking action because of the negative information you have collected.

☆☆☆☆☆

These are the five steps of the thinking process we all use whenever we buy something. When you attempt to persuade someone, you must communicate in terms of this thinking process. *Feed those steps properly, and you are likely to be persuasive. Frustrate them, and failure is guaranteed.*

A good way to learn how to judge how others use this process is to observe your own behavior. Remember, the order of the steps is important. We move through these steps in this order every time. The process can be very slow. You may repeat or redo certain steps. For example, when you try to make a decision, you may find a gap in your information that sends you back to the search step. After you redo the search, you will move through evaluation again and then on to decision making. You may go back and forth, but the order is the same.

Your experience will vary. Today you may move straight through the five steps. On other occasions you may end the process early, because your search fails to come up with anything worth evaluating. Another time, just as you are making a decision to buy or not to buy, a new piece of information may appear that causes you to reevaluate. However your thinking proceeds, you will find the process orderly. You will be aware of your position at all times.

As you observe your own behavior, you will become sensitive to that of others. Your observations of the buying process in yourself and others will build a reservoir of useful experience. Your persuasion skills will become more effective. You can depend on this phase of human behavior. It is rock-solid.

Sometimes, however, the process can be difficult to identify. In every seminar we give, a few participants ask if there are not exceptions to this buying process. Most people become clearly aware of their own five-step behavior when the buying process is slow, as it usually is when it involves buying a home or a car or choosing colleges for one's children. The so-called impulse purchase is frequently cited as a possible exception because it seems different from other purchases. This is when you set out to buy something specific and come away having added "on impulse" one or more seemingly unplanned items. It is as though some sudden, external force prompted an involuntary action on your part.

Actually, there is no difference in the process itself. In this case, it just works faster. Consider this scenario. You are at work. You came in early that morning to catch up on some emergency work. It is now mid-afternoon. You have been working straight through since 7 A.M. You *need* a break to relieve your stress. You decide that a few minutes with the sports page will help. You head for the newsstand to get a paper.

Upon arrival you realize how tired you are. You remember that you forgot to eat lunch. Obviously, your blood sugar is low, and you need a pickup of some kind. Dinner is hours away, and you *recognize* your need for a pickup as being immediate. A quick shot of sugar should do the trick. You *search* the store and notice candy bars. You scan the brands, *evaluate, decide,* and walk out with both the newspaper and the candy bar, the item that some people would call the impulse purchase. All this happens in less than a minute compared with the days or weeks you spend when buying something big like a home. But the candy was not an unplanned purchase; nor was it involuntary. It seemed sudden only because you became aware of an existing condition (fatigue) and recognized an existing need that required immediate attention.

Charlie, one of a dozen participants in a recent seminar, said he was ready to buy into the five-step idea but for one exception. To explain this, he asked that we project the five steps again on the screen: NEED, RECOGNITION, SEARCH, EVALUATION, DECISION. Looking at the screen, I asked Charlie to tell us about the exception.

"It's my wife," he said with a note of exasperation.

This got the immediate attention of Linda, who focused tightly on Charlie.

"What about your wife, Charlie?" she asked, clipping her words.

"My wife, Marie, defies all these steps. Marie goes out and buys many clothes, brings them home, and then takes most of them back the next day. I think that's an exception."

Before I could respond, Linda took the lead by stepping to the front of the room. As she pointed to the words on the screen, she said, "Charlie, some women have NEEDS to spend money and you should RECOGNIZE that."

We all laughed, including Charlie, but that did not take care of the issue of whether Charlie's wife's behavior was an exception.

During further discussion it developed that when she got the new merchandise home, Marie would mix and match the old with the new. Charlie finally decided that his wife's habit of bringing merchandise home was really part of her *evaluation* and *decision* steps. She could not decide in the store how the new things would go with her existing wardrobe. Charlie therefore agreed that Marie's behavior fit the pattern and was not an exception.

The Linda-Charlie exchange is important because it makes clear that it is not always easy for one person to identify someone else's process. In this case, though the process was there, Charlie needed a few extra minutes of thought to identify it. Most books, lectures, and seminars about persuasion emphasize buyers' needs, but few explain the mechanism that tells you why this is so vitally important. Without this insight, any persuasion effort is operating blindly.

If, by now, you agree that this is the process you use when making a buying decision, you can also agree that this is the way others do their buying too. So, if you want to persuade people or motivate them to do something, you must find a way to take them through this five-step process.

These five steps represent your target when you are aiming at a specific persuasion task. This is the process you must influence. It is your target. Therefore, it deserves your full attention and study. The process has all the features of any target; sometimes it is stationary and well defined; sometimes it moves or changes character and shape; it may disappear forever or reappear in a new shape, and so on. *Feed those steps properly and you are most likely to succeed. Frustrate them, and failure is guaranteed.*

Our task, then, is to find a reliable method of meshing our persuasive messages with the thinking process of the buying mind. There are selling formulas and selling formulas. Most do not deserve your time or attention. For example, let's look at one of the most popular. It appears sound at first glance, but it really has little merit. It is called AIDA. The idea is that when selling you must get people's **A**ttention, develop their **I**nterest, stimulate their **D**esire, and force some kind of **A**ction. One disqualifying fault with this formula is that it has no basis. It is not predicated on the behavior of the buying mind.

Another fault is that it does not bear analysis. What do we mean by *attention*? How do we quantify it? How do we decide when we have it? You and I could throw a brick through a store window and get attention. How do we measure and define *interest* and *desire*? How much of each of these does the seller have to generate in the buyer to get the desired results? *Action* poses another dilemma. The formula does not ask us to define the intended outcome before we start. So, if we do not know what action we are trying to get, how will we know what action to request?

The disqualifying faults with most selling techniques are these three:

1. They do not mesh and interact efficiently with the mental process of the buying mind.
2. They will not stand up under the critical analysis necessary in today's sophisticated and competitive world.
3. They emphasize interpersonal skills over analytical thinking skills.

"Think first" is still the best rule.

Now that you are conscious of the mental mechanism that guides people through the buying process, you are ready to learn how to influence that mechanism. Your need is to approach the persuasion task on an interactive, analytical basis. Solid, well-defined messages are required by most technical, professional, manufacturing, research, sales, marketing, and management people in the work force today.

We will do it with the second of the two thinking processes. To repeat, this is a step-by-step, analytical thinking process to help you organize and present information in a logical, persuasive manner that meshes and interacts with the first thinking process of the buying mind (NEEDS, RECOGNITION, SEARCH, EVALUATION, DECISION). Use of these logical principles will build a lifetime skill that will give you an important edge in your ability to persuade and motivate others.

5

The Persuasion Process: Part I

The second of the two thinking processes is the foundation of the persuasion skill you can use for the rest of your life. It meshes and interacts with the thinking process of the buying mind that you learned about in Chapter 4.

As a refresher, let's recap what the first thinking process involved. If you frustrate the buying process in someone, you end the persuasion process right then. Anytime you doubt the ironclad validity of this truth, think of your own justified, negative reaction when someone ignores your RECOGNIZED NEEDS, inhibits your SEARCH, shortcuts your EVALUATION, or pressures you into a DECISION.

Now let's look at the second part of the persuasion process. This, the method you can use to get others to take the actions you request, is a logical discipline. Easy to understand and remember, it is the basis of a lifetime skill. There are eight steps.

The First Five Steps of the Persuasion Process

The first five of these steps make up the main structure of the persuasion process and are presented and demonstrated in this chapter. The other three steps will help you control your persuasion process. They will be presented in Chapter 8 after you have a firm grounding in the main structure.

1. NEEDS: You start by establishing the needs of your audience. If possible, you get agreement that the needs, as you understand them, are accurate. Avoid misunderstandings about the nature of these needs at all costs.
2. PLAN: Next you propose a plan of action that will satisfy the established needs. This should be a descriptive statement of twenty-five words or less.
3. HOW-IT-WORKS: At this point you explain how your proposed plan will be carried out. Include only enough information to ensure that the person understands the workings of your plan in principle.
4. RESULTS: This is the payoff for your audience. You describe how the results, or benefits, of your proposed plan will satisfy each of your audience's needs as established at the outset.
5. NEXT STEP: Finally, you ask your audience to take the action your plan requires and to do it by a specified time.

This is the structure. You may feel that it is oversimplified. It is not. Successful proposals follow this form. This is because such proposals mesh and interact with the thinking process we all use when we make a buying decision. Even proposals involving the most complex subject matter can and should be reduced to these five steps.

Demonstration

Let's go through this structure again. This time we will assume a role and create a proposal addressed to the Green Valley Country Club. *Our role:* We are marketers of computer systems designed for country clubs. One of our products, the Point-of-Sale System, is designed to automate food and beverage service. Our objective is to sell the Point-of-Sale System to this club and get it installed within forty-five days.

The person we must persuade, our audience, is the recently elected club president, Jeffrey Smith. A lawyer, he is a relatively new member of the club and was elected to the board for the first time only last year.

Smith's assertiveness has caused the club manager, Michael Brown, to back off from his usual leadership position. Incidentally, Brown wanted to buy our system a year ago, but the previous president turned it down. Too expensive! We believe that Brown is on our side. To keep it that way, our tactic is to deal directly with Smith but to keep Brown "in the loop" at all times. This means that we will keep him informed and try to have him included in every meeting we have with Smith.

In preparation, we meet with Smith (and Brown) to establish the needs of the club as Smith sees them and, of course, to size up the man himself. We spend most of the time listening to Smith's responses to our questions. During our meeting, he makes one point abundantly clear: He watches the dollars very carefully and operates on a tight budget. Smith emphasizes the point by describing himself as "thrifty." Brown comments later that the word *cheap* would be a more accurate description.

We get a strong impression that Smith wants to make his presence as the new president felt promptly. At 40, he is a partner in a local, up-and-coming law firm. He comes off as a well-organized, ego-driven "doer" with a strong, personal agenda. Our guess is that he wishes to impress certain of the club's influential members who could become lucrative clients. One way he could do this would be to make a noticeable positive change soon after taking office. Although he is new as president, we believe Smith has enough clout to get prompt approval from the board of governors if he decides to buy our product. We discount his "thrifty" comment and believe he will buy if a proposal seems economically sound and fits his personal agenda. In doing this he could send a positive message to the membership about the quality of his "leadership" and make substantial claims for himself as a problem solver who can save money, improve the club's efficiency, and simultaneously improve service for the members.*

This club uses a manual system to write up, fill, and charge

---

*Sometimes a good way to win favorable attention is to restore rather than to create anew. The idea is to avoid change, because people often resist it. Smith may know this. If this is Smith's tactic, he will get "applause" by restoring the good food and beverage service the club delivered in the "old" days.

all food and beverage orders. The waiting and kitchen personnel make mistakes constantly. These cause delays. The quality of service suffers. Mistakes also lead to costly losses. These occur when orders are filled but not billed and when chits are lost or credited to the wrong members. In addition, the office people spend sixty hours or more per week handling thousands of chits. They do all this by hand. The work includes rechecking arithmetic and keying the information into the club's computer. Sometimes the clerical load is so heavy that it delays the mailing of monthly bills to members. This hurts the cash flow. Everyone agrees that the current process induces errors and consequent losses. Smith believes that a loss of about 5 percent on sales of $600,000 per year is a reasonable estimate of the damage the current system inflicts.

Developing Our Proposal in Outline Form

1. NEEDS: To start our proposal, we summarize the club's NEEDS as we believe Jeffrey Smith sees them:

- Reduce the time, cost, and errors of writing up food and beverage orders at the point of sale.
- Eliminate poor service caused by order-writing errors and thereby restore the good service enjoyed when the club was smaller.
- Improve efficiency and order handling in the kitchen.
- Stop billing errors to members.
- Cut drastically the high clerical costs involved in the process.
- Find ready-made, cost-effective solutions to solve long-standing club problems quickly.
- Be sure that any new program is likely to be acceptable to the members. (Dealing with complaining members is the most unpleasant part of Smith's job as president.)
- Get a solution in place and running within thirty days of decision.

2. PLAN: Our PLAN statement tells Smith what we think he should do to satisfy the club's needs:

- We propose that the club install our computerized Point-of-Sale System.

3. HOW-IT-WORKS: Our HIW step describes how the Point-of-Sale System will work:

- The System allows the wait staff to enter table and bar orders quickly and accurately.
- It avoids "error" losses that currently amount to 5 percent of total billings.
- It provides clear orders for the kitchen.
- It prints easy-to-read checks for members and enters correct data automatically in the existing computer for billing.
- It sets prices, produces menus, provides ingredient usage reports and menu sales analysis, and tracks costs.
- It verifies any order when required.
- The price is $27,000, complete.
- There is a twelve-month warranty.

4. RESULTS: Our RESULTS step describes the benefits the club will receive as the result of installing the Point-of-Sale System:

- Dramatically reduced time, cost, and errors connected with food and beverage order taking at point of sale
- Immediate improvement of service to members
- Elimination of clerical costs and the diversion of personnel to other tasks. Savings will be equivalent to the cost of one person working full-time.
- The System will pay for itself in about eleven months. Savings will be approximately $30,000 per year (5 percent of $600,000 in annual food and beverage billings).
- No more problems with incorrect billings or other clerical errors, thus reducing club member complaints
- A bug-free system guaranteed to work the first time around
- Only one hour needed to train club personnel in the use of the Point-of-Sale System

5. NEXT STEP: Our NEXT STEP asks Smith for a specific action by a specific time:

- If you will have your office place an order for our Point-of-Sale System this week, we can have it running by the end of the month. This includes training all your people.

Delivery

Now that the outline form is complete, your thinking has been done. All you need to do is convert it to an appropriate delivery mode that best suits the situation and present it to Jeffrey Smith. There are three possibilities:

1. Do a fifteen-minute oral presentation using the outline on an overhead projector or chart pad. Also supply a written proposal as a leave-behind.
2. Convert the outline into a written proposal (letter) of one or two pages at the most and let it stand on its own.
3. Deliver the proposal as a one-on-one oral presentation without visual aids. Use the outline or the written proposal as a leave-behind or as a follow-up.

We took option 1 because we wanted another personal contact with Smith and because he requested a written proposal for his presentation to the board of governors. On the basis of the outline, we prepared a one-page proposal in letter form as a leave-behind (see Figure 5-1).

☆☆☆☆☆

You now know the structures of the persuasion process, namely the two thinking processes involved. These are your tools. This gives you a sense of the fundamental principles of the persuasion process. Here, with the two processes side by side in chart form, you can see how they function together. When you present your proposals according to the five steps of the seller's process, your message will mesh and interact effectively with

Figure 5-1. The Green Valley Country Club proposal in letter form.

Green Valley
Country Club

Dear Mr. Smith:

To summarize my meeting with you and your manager, I understand that the Green Valley Country Club wants to do the following concerning its food and beverage service:

- Reduce the time, cost, and errors involved in handling orders.
- Eliminate poor service caused by errors and slowness.
- Improve efficiency of order handling in the kitchen.
- Stop billing errors to members.
- Cut clerical costs through computerization.
- Find a ready-made, cost-effective, tested system that is salable to Club members.
- Complete the task within thirty days of making a decision.

To meet these needs, I propose that the Club install our Point-of-Sale System. Here is how our proposal works and what the System does:

Using our computerized System, your servers will write and enter orders quickly and accurately. Kitchen personnel will receive printed orders, ranked for prompt, first-come-first-served, error-free handling. Through automation, the System will allow serving personnel to speed delivery and present members with legible checks containing correct prices and totals.

All charges will be posted immediately and automatically in the Club's computer for accurate billing. No clerical work is needed. When required by a member, office personnel can verify any billing in less than one minute.

The System will automatically change prices, produce menus, and provide ingredient usage reports and menu sales analysis. Service, kitchen, and office personnel can be trained to use the System in one hour.

You can have the System installed and running in thirty days from our receipt of your order. The price is $27,000, including a one-year warranty and training of your staff.

Results for the Green Valley Country Club

With the Point-of-Sale System in place, you and your members will notice an immediate improvement in service because the time required to process orders will be reduced. Errors in both orders and billing will decrease by 95 percent. You will cut clerical costs by the salary of one full-time person. The savings from reducing losses and errors will pay for the System in eleven months. After that you will save $30,000 per year, every year (5 percent of $600,000 in annual billings). You can be sure of the project's success because our System has been tested and proved in other clubs. Your members will be delighted with the service and savings. You can have the System up and running with a one-year warranty within twenty days of your order.

If your office places an order with us next week, we can have the System in full operation by month's end. Many thanks for your time and interest. I will call you Friday.

Cordially,

Harry L. Stephens

the buyer's process. You can depend on it, period! And you can see why frustrating the buyer's process will quickly kill any persuasion effort. Suggestion: Commit this chart to memory.

Buyer's Process		Seller's Process
	←	
• NEEDS and RECOGNITION	←	• NEEDS
• SEARCH	←	• PLAN
• EVALUATION	←	• HOW-IT-WORKS and RESULTS (Benefits)
• DECISION	←	• NEXT STEP

We wish we could tell you that persuasion skills are simple and easy to acquire. We cannot because some persuasion tasks become frightfully complicated. Take heart. The two thinking processes you have learned so far will guide you through the most challenging tasks. You can rely on them as your reference point on this aspect of human behavior. They will not change in principle. Only the details will change. With this as a foundation, you can move ahead well equipped to refine your tools and learn more about their uses.

6

Needs

Of the five steps in *The Anatomy of Persuasion* process, the most important is NEEDS. No single part of the process deserves more of your attention and study. Your ability to discover and interpret the needs of others is essential to your success. This is not an easy task. The study of needs is just as complex as the study of human behavior because human needs are the motivators of human behavior. Understanding the mechanisms will help you immeasurably.

If we were to visualize the needs and drives of any person as a body of information residing in the mind, we might imagine a static collection of discrete thoughts and ideas stored conveniently in one place, each independent of the others and ready to come into play as required. An analogy might be a workshop full of tools, each having a specific nature and use but not having much relationship to one another. Except that they share the common denomination of tools, the hammer is not related to the saw or the saw to the pliers, and so on. Nor does one tool influence the shape, size, value, function, or importance of the others. When you need a screwdriver, nothing else will do. Each tool does its unchanging thing when called upon, period. When the screwdriver is in use, the value of the hammer remains unchanged, although it may not be needed at that moment. Unfortunately, the collection of needs residing in our minds does not operate in this fashion.

Instead, visualize needs and drives as a dynamic, interrelated, and intertwined collection of thoughts, ideas, and motivations that direct our decisions and actions. These are in constant flux, moving up and down the scale of priorities, each changing in value and each influencing the value and importance of all the others. A given need may grow to occupy space left by another, or it may diminish in importance and value to make room for another whose moment has come. One need may be the top priority now with fulfillment in progress. Suddenly something changes and everything stops. Fulfillment efforts are instantly postponed or canceled. A new need reaches ascendancy and displaces the old. The person's focus changes and he or she reorders all other needs in terms of their current value and importance. When a need is satisfied, refocusing and reordering occur again. Our task then is to deal with a complex, ever-changing matrix of needs. Identifying and defining needs is our next task.

Conscious Needs and Basic Needs

As a first cut, we can divide the whole body of needs into two main groups: *conscious needs* and *basic needs*. One way to distinguish between them is by the way we treat them (or by the way they treat us).

Conscious needs are usually talked about, written about, and discussed openly and freely by those involved. People talk about their need for housing, new clothes, cosmetics, vacations, getting a degree or a boat or a car, cutting costs, improving product quality or profitability or market share, and so on. Conscious needs change frequently, depending on the issues at hand and the priority of the moment.

Basic needs never change. They are innate and identical for all human beings. Basic needs are our psychological underpinnings. They are *not* usually talked about, written about, or discussed openly and freely by the people involved. People almost never talk about their own need for self-esteem, for freedom from fear, for love, strength, adequacy, status, and so on. Such needs are highly personal, very private, and deeply seated. In fact, most people are not fully aware of their basic needs, but they do respond to them promptly and specifically.

Conscious needs are always manifestations of basic needs.

They are inseparable in one sense. They reside in the same person, and they work together. For an analogy, think of a flowering plant. Conscious needs are visible, clear, and out in the open like the blossoms, leaves, and stems. We talk about them openly. Basic needs are the root systems below ground and out of sight. We seldom talk about them, although they support the plant physically, feed it, and govern its behavior. Conscious needs are the surface indicators of what is really happening within the person. For example, you probably know people who have bought a certain make of luxury automobile not for its features but for the status it conferred. As these people talk openly of safety, reliability, comfort, and durability, they silently feed their self-esteem with the status value they believe such cars offer.

Most persuasion tasks involve conscious needs rather than the basic needs that prompt them, because these are the things we can talk about. We can usually take conscious needs at their face value and succeed with persuasion efforts based on these alone. There are times, however, when we are stopped by an objection, obstruction, rejection, or some other barrier. This is when we need our knowledge of basic needs, the root system below ground, to help us analyze and interpret the underlying causes, find solutions, and restore progress.

Fortunately, we do not have to reinvent the wheel. The late psychologist, Abraham H. Maslow, developed an extremely useful map of fundamental human needs that he called "The Basic Needs Hierarchy."[*] Maslow's ideas provide us with a broad means of interpreting, stimulating, and influencing the behavior of others. He presented five levels of needs and arranged them in order of rank, with physiological needs as the lowest and most important in the hierarchy. A basic need becomes active only after those below it in the hierarchy, that is, of greater rank, have been satisfied. A lower basic need can preempt a higher one. For example, a person engaged in satisfying a higher level of need would immediately redirect his efforts if a lower-level, more important need suddenly became unsatisfied. Maslow's pyramidal hierarchy is seen in Figure 6-1.

[*]See Abraham H. Maslow, *Motivation and Personality*, 3d ed. (New York: Harper Collins, 1987).

Figure 6-1. Maslow's basic needs hierarchy.

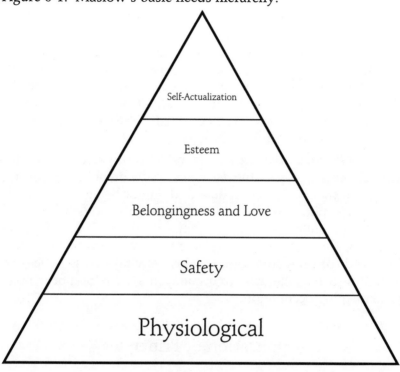

The Basic Needs Hierarchy

1. *Physiological needs:* These are the physical needs a person has to maintain a normal state. They include the need for food, water, shelter, and everything else that is required to sustain physical well-being. Only when the physiological needs are satisfied will the higher-level needs come into play.

2. *Safety needs:* These have to do with the need for security, stability, and protection; the need to be free from fear, anxiety, chaos, disturbance of the status quo, or burnout; the need for law and order, structure, and the like. When one's safety is threatened, practically everything else seems less important.

3. *Belongingness and love needs:* These have to do with the need for personal relationships—with parents, a spouse, children, relatives, or friends—for a place in a group or family. We

hunger for affectionate relationships with people in general. This can account for our affinity for clubs, associations, "gangs," and the like.

4. *Esteem needs:* These are the needs people have to gain and maintain high evaluations of themselves—self-respect or self-esteem and the esteem of others. Included here too are the desires for strength, achievement, competence, and self-confidence. Our need for esteem can be satisfied by recognition, fame, glory, prestige, or status.

5. *Self-actualization need:* This refers to a person's need for self-fulfillment, namely the drive to actually do or become everything that that person is capable of doing or being. This need is particularly noticeable in top sports personalities such as professional tour golfers and tennis players who milk dry their reserves of mental and physical energy to win top-rated events. The need for self-actualization is just as vital in less noticeable activities such as the drive to become an ideal parent or to excel in some other occupation.

Application of Principles

In most persuasion tasks, addressing conscious needs is enough. We rarely have to go deeper. But our knowledge of basic needs can be of immeasurable help when a proposal is rejected or stalls for any of a number of reasons: indecision, unforeseen objections, a change in conditions such as another activity that preoccupies the audience. At times like these we need extra insight to guide us in our persuasion task.

Return to Green Valley

To see how conscious and basic needs come into play, let's go back to Jeffrey Smith, the recently elected president of the Green Valley Country Club. Our proposal for the Point-of-Sale System dealt only with his conscious needs for the club. These were about reducing the time, cost, and errors of writing food and beverage orders at the point of sale, eliminating poor service caused by order-writing errors, and so on. You will recall our impression of

Smith as an ego-driven man with a strong personal agenda. We guessed that his purpose was to favorably impress certain of the club's members so as to attract them to his law firm as clients. Had we judged Smith's activity according to his basic needs, we would have placed him at level four (Esteem), particularly because we saw him as seeking the esteem of others.

The structure of our proposal, however, did not consider his basic needs, because it seemed sufficient to structure the proposal around his conscious needs. This proved to be sound because we got the order for the Point-of-Sale System and started working with the club manager and staff on the complicated details of filling it. We enjoyed a cordial working relationship with all the people at the club, and the work was going well.

One day, out of the blue, Michael Brown told us that Smith had put the project on hold. We were to stop all work until further notice. We probed for an explanation. At first, Brown refused to tell us what was happening. Finally, and reluctantly, he informed us in strict confidence that an employee had sued the club for gender discrimination. It seems that Brown, acting under Smith's unofficial orders, promoted a male employee to the job of head chef, following which a female employee, claiming that she was more qualified for the job, sued.

Smith had decided to keep the matter superconfidential and to stall for time. The woman's lawyer, disliking Smith's tactics, leaked the story to the local papers. Smith was caught flat-footed because the club members had not been informed of the promotion or of its consequences. Worse, Smith had not involved the board in the decision.

All hell broke loose for Smith; his phone rang endlessly. Many influential club members were angry and vocal. They told Smith that "his" board should have foreseen and prevented the problem from arising in the first place, and, in the second place, that he should have handled it quietly. The members resented hearing about the matter through the newspapers rather than through the club. Members of the board also took flak and lost no time in advising Smith of their displeasure. Smith was grievously embarrassed both as president of the club and as a lawyer. He considered the situation to be out of hand. In short, it was a debacle. The club manager went on to tell us that Smith wanted to concentrate on the lawsuit personally and would not be able to give time to the Point-of-Sale project until later. We were stopped dead in our tracks and very much concerned.

Interruptions like this can put any incomplete transaction at risk. As the Smith saga unfolded, the club manager, fortunately, kept us in touch with developments. Our knowledge of basic needs gave us useful insights. We were able not only to interpret the action but also to *predict* in a broad way what Smith was likely to do. These same insights helped us save our sale when Smith put it at risk again in a last-minute turn of events. Here is what happened.

Smith had been operating in line with level-four needs (Esteem). When the lawsuit disturbed the peace and good order of the club, it created a need for action by Smith at the second level (Safety). Preempting his own fourth-level activities, he dropped to the second level (Safety). He ended the gender discrimination complaint by promoting the woman to food service manager, a new job of equal rank to the chef's. Smith sent a letter to members announcing a prompt and amicable settlement. His law firm's public relations people placed that story in the newspapers without delay.

Some people might work at both levels simultaneously. Others, like Smith, will postpone one thing to attend to another, depending on their needs. In this case, the Point-of-Sale project could be set aside easily. The Club could continue with its present system for a while longer without a problem. More than that, Smith's time, constrained by a busy law practice, had other demands on it.

With his second-level needs (Safety) satisfied, Smith's efforts *predictably* returned to his level-four needs (Esteem). He must have felt personally tarred by the incident because he did something remedial. He smoothed matters over with an innovative, preventive program. Smith announced that he would present a seminar called "Law for Managers: How to Avoid Gender Discrimination." He ordered the club manager and his supervisors to attend. Smith also ordered the club manager to invite members of the board and committee people by personal phone call and to send written invitations to all club members. Special requests from outsiders also would be considered.

To avoid more bungling on communications, Smith called on his own public relations people again, this time to stage the entire event. The seminar was well promoted, well attended, well done, and well publicized—a professional job in all respects. In the end, Smith deodorized himself by its success. He came off operating at level four (Esteem) as an effective president who could fix problems and take preventive action.

At this point, we believed that Smith was beyond his problems, and our time had come to move ahead and install the Point-of-Sale System. Not so. Smith found himself at risk again. He discovered that no one had collected competitive bids for the Point-of-Sale System. A question about this would certainly come up at the annual meeting. Thus he faced another potential embarrassment. Once more, Smith *predictably* dipped down to level two (Safety) and took action to avoid being caught flat-footed again. Smith told the club manager to get bids from other suppliers. This put us at risk because our prices typically are higher than those of our competitors.

Our knowledge of basic needs, together with our observations of Smith's behavior as he shuttled between the two levels of basic needs, gave us a good idea of how we might preserve our business opportunity in spite of our higher prices. To meet the level-four (Esteem) needs of country club officials like Smith, we offset price differences with a special program that we created specifically for this purpose. It is a professionally packaged Publicity and Promotion Program (PPP) developed for our Point-of-Sale System. It meets the unspoken esteem needs of board members and presidents of clubs. It does a good job at gaining acceptance for the System and forestalling the inevitable critics and complainers that plague boards and committees in every club. We have used it successfully to offset price differences of up to 10 percent.

Because PPP is a costly item, we offer it only under special circumstances. PPP is a fully customized program that includes brochures, letters to members, and videos for use in the club. We put on a special live presentation for full membership meetings. We do press releases for print and broadcast media. PPP heaps credit on the club president, board members, the club manager, and any others who require stroking. The mere hint of "limelight" usually gets immediate and positive attention from the majority of board members, who welcome peer recognition. Such people find it easy to rationalize our slightly higher prices.

With this and Smith's agenda in mind, we asked for another audience with Smith to present PPP. We presented it as something new to meet the need (conscious needs) expressed by many clubs to do an effective job of "selling" the new Point-of-Sale System to the members, who, after all, will ultimately pay the bill. Smith bought into the PPP with appropriate enthusiasm. We had hit his basic needs at level four (Esteem) and preserved the business opportunity. We had guessed right about Smith, thanks to our knowledge of basic needs.

Conclusion

In developing needs in any situation, you must seek out conscious needs first. Most of the time, that will be enough. When it is not, study the applicable basic needs. Recall the flowering plant. Conscious needs are visible parts, the blossoms, leaves, buds, and stems. Basic needs, the invisible root parts, are the indicators of what is really happening within the person to control and prompt conscious needs. As you work at this, bear in mind that your experience is cumulative. You will gain verifiable insights and serviceable truths about the behavior of people. Your skill will go up and up and up. When you can recognize and fill both conscious and basic needs with the same message, you will be able to launch especially powerful persuasive thrusts. Here are two examples:

1. Our Publicity and Promotion Program (PPP) used to acquaint a club's members with the newly installed Point-of-Sale System, did that by combining the board's conscious need to gain the members' acceptance of the new system with the basic need, for esteem, of Smith and his board members.

2. In real life, Mercedes-Benz advertising skillfully combines the two needs by helping prospective buyers "justify" their extravagances. The ad introducing the new E-Class (expensive) models first presented the features: a newly designed body that will "look good ten years from now," quick acceleration

from 0 to 60 mph, safety technology, and so forth. This was followed by this powerful line, "It seems the new Mercedes-Benz E-Class is not a purchase driven by vanity, but one driven by reason."

☆☆☆☆☆

Of the five steps in *The Anatomy of Persuasion* process, the most important is NEEDS. No single part of the process deserves more of your attention and study.

7

The Persuasion Process: Part II

When we want to persuade people, we know we must influence the five-step buying process—needs, recognition, search, evaluation, decision. You have learned a way to make this happen with a five-step persuasion process that meshes and interacts with the buying process and will cause people to take the actions you propose. Although these steps are straightforward, clear, and easy to describe, successful application requires additional study of their use. As you learn more, you will notice immediate improvements in your personal skills.

Another Look at the Five Steps of the Persuasion Process

Needs

Start by establishing the needs of your audience. These can be recognized or unrecognized, conscious or unconscious. This is crucial and mandatory. If at all possible, get agreement that your understanding of the needs is accurate. At all costs, avoid misunderstanding as to what is required.

Your Skill Improvements

You will improve your ability to question, listen, remember, and analyze. You will think in terms of both the conscious needs

58

and the basic needs of the audience you have in mind. You will become attuned to expressions of need that may once have passed unnoticed in the flow of conversation. This is called *selective perception.*

Think of the last time you considered buying a new car. You became interested in a certain model. Once you had examined the car in the showroom, you developed a special recognition for it. After that, as you drove through traffic, you found yourself picking out that model from the hundreds of others you passed. The same thing will happen with your ability to recognize needs.

You will become more incisive. As your recognition ability grows, you will learn to ask leading questions about needs. Your powers of observation will increase. Thus you will identify needs and make innovative connections more quickly. You will analyze and process this kind of information rapidly and effectively and operate with a high level of expertise. In short, you will learn to put yourself in the other person's place. If there is one word for all this, it is *empathy.* Learning to be empathic is vital.

There remains one question. How do you find out about another person's needs? You collect information carefully. You *ask* questions: who, where, what, when, why, how, and how much? You *observe.* You *listen.* You *read.* You *research.* You *remember.* And you *analyze.* Your skills will develop naturally and promptly. The fastest way to gain proficiency is to practice by preparing proposals. Practice! Practice! Practice!

Remember! *If for any reason you cannot identify and confirm your audience's needs, stop or delay your persuasion efforts until you can.* Once I made a presentation based on hearsay information about the needs of my audience. I should have known better. When finished, I asked the man for his reaction. "Like ships that pass in the night," he said. "You people didn't find out about our needs." I was dead in the water, wallowing in my own stupidity. Fortunately, I was granted a second try, and that was successful. Sorting out the needs requires careful examination and thoughtful analysis.

As you know by now, the subject of needs, as a topic for thought or discussion, is vast and complex, almost without end. What follows is intended only to help you start concentrating your thinking on the subject. With focus that comes with practice, you can gain insight and penetrate beyond the obvious. Here are a few ideas to help you start thinking about the needs of other people.

Economic Needs

Economic needs are important to most people. In business, they talk of lower costs, higher return on investment, improved productivity, increased profits, sales, market share, and the like. Personal economic needs might have to do with wages, salaries, bonuses, savings, loans, investments, tax liabilities, mortgages, or school and college expenses. These kinds of economic needs are usually reasonable, uncomplicated, and easy to understand and explain.

Then there are people with money hang-ups. As you think about them, you may decide that some of these hang-ups are symptomatic overlays for basic needs. Some older people think that accepting senior-citizen discounts tarnishes their image. Are these sometimes the same people who have a fetish about turning out lights? They will live in semidarkness to save a few pennies on electricity and then splurge on the most expensive brands of wine and liquor for personal consumption. What does this tell you?

Most people hate to pay "too much" for something. You probably know someone who drives ten miles out of his way to buy gasoline for a penny or two less per gallon, ignoring the fact that the cost of the extra mileage more than offsets the savings. Some people will do almost anything to get a bargain. It's a game with an unlimited number of participants who remain in constant touch and on full alert. One observer believes that there is more communication about bargains than there is about sports. Some people love to dicker over price. The combat with car dealers is more rewarding than the few hundred dollars that may have been saved. Others refuse to participate in such activity.

Hidden Needs

Some people have hidden needs they can't or won't talk about. These needs are elusive and sometimes very difficult, if not impossible, to identify and handle. A hidden need is often the desire to keep confidential something that might come up in the discussion of a proposal. People don't want to reveal such things as pending job changes, marriages, divorces, or illness. Perhaps there is a need to keep secret the news of a new program or policy, a merger, pending litigation, an acquisition, the resignation, demotion, or firing of an important person in the organization, even a scandal. The main thing is for you to know that hidden needs (and hidden objections) often exist and can become serious barriers. When rejection is inexplicable or merely unreasonable, a hidden need may be the cause.

Two friends of mine at DuPont who were selling polyester fibers as a replacement for cotton described how they uncovered a hidden need of the purchasing director, Joe Hunter, at a uniform rental company. The aim was to get Joe to buy uniforms made with a 65-35 percent Dacron* polyester-cotton blend. The Dacron uniforms looked better than those made of cotton. They cost 50 percent more but lasted twice as long. Joe's cotton uniforms had to be replaced every year. The polyester-cotton blend would last two years. Joe's annual budget to replace worn cotton uniforms was $500,000. The cost of buying polyester-cotton uniforms initially would be $750,000. Annualized, however, the new uniforms would cost $375,000 or 25 percent less than the cotton ones. Good deal? Yes, on the face of it, but Joe would not buy in. He kept putting off the decision in spite of the facts. Although my friends were perplexed, they were experienced people and recognized that Joe probably had a hidden need.

After much skillful and delicate probing, Joe finally, and very reluctantly, revealed that he had been working with his boss on a new incentive compensation program to help control costs. It would tie managers' bonuses to their budgets. The idea was to reduce tendencies to overrun budgets. Consequently, the mere suggestion of overrunning his own $500,000 uniform budget would undermine the new program before it got started. Joe was embarrassed by his own shortsightedness. Worse, he thought his boss would be too, because in all their planning, neither one of them had thought beyond one-year budgeting.

*Dacron is a registered trademark of the DuPont Company.

The new program was still superconfidential. He was taking a risk even talking about it. Therefore, Joe's need, hidden up to now, was for a way to get his boss to adjust the new bonus system before he dared propose a budget overrun. Joe had not figured out a way to do this without disturbing the new incentive compensation program. With the hidden need uncovered, the DuPont people, working with Joe, were able to come up with a proposal to include multiyear budgets and still keep the new incentive program intact. Joe sold the idea to his boss.

Hidden needs come in many "invisible" forms. There is no ready formula for identifying them or coping with them once they are identified. Most people have something to hide. Sometimes people can be brought around when they recognize that there is something in it for them. Persistent digging is often required. Even so, some hidden needs remain overwhelming obstacles.

Awakening Needs

Some needs must be awakened. This is not always an easy task. Technology is almost always well ahead of popular acceptance, as are revolutionary ideas. Just because something new comes along that allows us to do something better, faster, cheaper, safer, easier, neater, cleaner does not ensure the product's immediate acceptance. More often than not, it ensures resistance because it represents unwanted change.

The virtues of doing the "impossible" elude most of us, because we seldom think about them. Only a relatively few years ago, the ability to do rapid, accurate mathematical calculations at any time was not a recognized need. People got along without it because lugging around a large, cumbersome, forty-pound calculating machine made the idea impractical. Even people who needed to do such calculations did them manually and tolerated the inevitable errors. Nobody yearned for an electronic calculator that would fit in one's pocket or handbag. Even after these handy devices appeared, people did not rush out and buy them by the millions as they do today. At first, these calculators were expensive. Slowly, over the years, as the cost came down and the value-in-use went up, the need was awakened. People recognized the value in having balanced checkbooks, in avoiding the hideous penalties of arithmetic mistakes on tax returns, and so on. Today most people would feel lost without having several calculators.

Likewise, awakening the need for antilock brake systems (ABS) in automobiles was a slow process. They were available for cars for twenty-five years before they became factory-installed options. Awakening needs is even more difficult when some people don't want them awakened. What about the resistance to seat belts in automobiles? These were first available commercially in the early 1950s. Even now some people will not use them.

The situation with personal computers (PCs) is similar. In the 1970s, mainframe computer manufacturers and corporate data processing managers had control of the hardware and software of management information systems. These people actually controlled the information flow. They decided what others in their organizations would and would not be allowed to have. They could manipulate whatever served their purposes. Their arrogance abounded. Such power gave these managers direct lines to the top of their organizations. They had it made, or thought they had.

As PCs appeared, resistance from mainframe computer manufacturers and corporate data processing managers became active and intense. The personal computer threatened their market, their power, and their positions. This resistance was amplified by computer people working within companies and government offices. But as people within these organizations learned to operate PCs, the mysteries of computers disappeared and PCs began to appear in homes and offices everywhere, much to the consternation of the once lofty data processing managers. The smart corporate data processing managers joined the trend to PCs. They wisely helped select the best PCs and trained their people to use the newest software. In short, they identified an awakening need and filled it. The other corporate data processing managers are working elsewhere.

Summary: You cannot proceed *safely* with your proposal task until you have met one essential condition, namely, identified the needs of your audience. In addition, you must make every effort to meet a second condition whenever possible: You must gain agreement from your audience that the identified needs can be acted on now.*

Plan

This should be a direct statement of twenty-five words or less that says exactly what you want your audience to do, *and nothing more:* Here are some examples of concise plan statements:

> "To satisfy your needs and those of your family, I propose that you buy the house we looked at on Maple Avenue."

> "To satisfy the needs of your company, I propose that you take our lease-purchase plan for ten High-Orbit computers."

> "To help meet your objectives, I propose that you approve this new budget."

Your Skill Improvements

You will enhance your ability to define the exact action you want your audience to take. As you practice this step, your thought processes will become much more precise and your ability to prepare concise PLAN statements will become second nature to you. Your audiences will have no doubt about the specific actions you propose. Your PLAN statements will be clear, bold, and unambiguous. Remember, your PLAN statement should not include any detail, such as the price of the house on Maple Avenue. Detail is covered in HOW-IT-WORKS.

Helpful Hint: Add a transition line at the end of your PLAN statement to move your audience's attention without hesitation to the next step, HOW-IT-WORKS. Here are some examples:

---

*Under certain circumstances, you may wish to make assumptions about the needs of your audience. Assuming needs can be a risky but a reasonable and justifiable action when: (1) You believe you have reliable background information about the needs of an individual for whom your proposal is intended, but you cannot contact that person in advance to verify your assumptions, (2) your audience is unknown to you but apparently has similar needs to people you do know, and (3) you are preparing an advertising campaign and are banking on the idea that enough people in the audience will have the needs your offer will satisfy, and will respond favorably to your message.

"To satisfy your needs and those of your family, I propose that you buy the house we looked at on Maple Avenue. *Let me explain why this will work out well for you.*"

"To satisfy the needs of your company, I propose that you take our lease-purchase plan for ten High-Orbit computers. *Here is how this proposal will work out.*"

"To help meet our objectives, I propose that you approve this new budget. *Please let me summarize the details.*"

How-It-Works

Here is where you explain how your proposed plan works. Once again, you want to keep your audience's attention moving without hesitation to the next step when the RESULTS (benefits) of your proposal will come alive. Include only enough information in HIW to ensure that your audience understands the workings of your PLAN in principle, *and nothing more.*

Your Skill Improvements

Your communicating skills will sharpen. You will learn to get to the heart of the matter much faster. You will learn to present the governing principles, leaving confusing details aside. This is where you can present material answering the who, where, when, why, how, and how much questions. Beware of hazards. Sifting out the unimportant from the important for someone else can be difficult. The temptation is to provide more information than is really necessary. But either too much or too little information can sidetrack your audience and cause you to lose control of the process midway through the selling process. So, how do you decide what is important and what isn't when you are trying to give your audience an understanding in principle?

First, develop all the information that would apply to the who, where, when, why, how, and how much questions. Do all your homework. Quantify the information you have collected— cost and price details, size, shape, quantity, availability, reliability, liability, warranty, time involved, competitive comparisons, regulations, end-user requirements, and so on. Qualify the information you develop with supporting data. If you have something to say about satisfied customers, be prepared to name them and to tell how satisfied they are. If you claim that the product meets government regulations, be prepared to provide supporting evidence.

Second, put yourself in your audience's place and decide what, among all the details, would be the absolute minimum you would need to make a decision. Then use only that much. Keep the rest as hip-pocket data in case you get a question about something you have not included.

If, as president of your company, you were being asked to approve a plan for a new multimillion-dollar plant, you would not want to be distracted by detailed information about the process the plant will use unless it is absolutely critical to the proposition. Sifting out detailed information is easier said than done when you are so involved. The bulk of this information is probably far more important and essential to you than it is to anyone else. In general, provide the bare essentials. Then be prepared to elaborate on points and/or answer questions. This technique ensures complete preparation, and it lowers the risk of having your audience get hung up on "irrelevant details" or, worse, turn off in the middle of your proposal. You might seek the opinion of a colleague on your proposal. Remember, everybody needs an editor.

Results

This is the payoff for your audience. You describe how the RE-SULTS (benefits) of your proposed plan will satisfy each of your audience's needs as established in the first step.

Your Skill Improvements

You will improve your ability to motivate others because you will learn to think, talk, and write in terms of *benefits,* or what's in it for the other person. This is something most people fail to do. To test this, just listen to what most people say. Very few use the power of benefits in their communications; most talk in terms of things instead of explaining what the things do. This is because most people do not know how to make that all-important translation.

Although Chapter 9 will be devoted to features, functions, and benefits, definitions are appropriate here. People buy ideas, products, and services not because of what these things *are* but because of what these things *do*. People want to know what's in it for them in terms of benefits that fill their needs as they see them.

Definition: A *feature* is a thing (product, service, idea). A *benefit* is what that thing (feature) will do for you or someone else. For example, an antilock brake system (ABS) in an automobile is a feature. Unless someone tells you what this thing will do for you, it is really a great big expensive nothing. It expresses no benefit to you. "So what!" you might say, shrugging your shoulders as the car salesperson wonders why the mere mention of an ABS doesn't turn you on.

But suppose the car salesperson tells you what the remarkable brake system will do for you. ABS will help you avoid those inevitable, terrifying, dangerous skids on wet or icy roads. You will avoid personal injury and costly damage to your car because you will stop faster and more surely under all conditions. And you won't need any special skill to make this happen. All you need to do is step on the brakes as usual and the system will provide all these benefits automatically. And, as a bonus benefit, because this brake system will reduce your risk of accident, your insurance company will reduce the cost of your insurance. In other words, there's a lot in it for you.

Benefits expressed in the RESULTS step tie in directly with satisfying the specific NEEDS established in your proposal. It is important to make certain that your audience thoroughly understands these RESULTS and how they satisfy those NEEDS.

This also is where you should present any bonus benefits that flow from your PLAN. These are the extras, the nice-to-have additions you may be able to include, like the bonus benefit mentioned above—a discount on the buyer's car insurance.

Next Step

Here is where you ask your audience to take the action your PLAN requires and to do it by a specified time.

Your Skill Improvements

You will improve your ability to get action because you will overcome the worst failing of people who try to be persuasive. They fail to ask for specific action by a specific time. You must ask your audience to make a decision to accept your PLAN. Somehow people resist taking this step. Sales managers will tell you that getting salespeople to ask for the order is difficult. We all fear the pain of rejection. We unconsciously try to avoid it. In spite of all our efforts to prepare and deliver a proposal, we all tend to hesitate just before asking for the order, just as some of us hesitate before diving into the swimming pool. If you don't ask for the action, you may not get it. So ask for *specific action* by a *specific time:* "Please sign this work request now, so we can complete the installation by next Wednesday."

☆☆☆☆☆

The Anatomy of Persuasion can become a lifetime tool for you. It will allow great flexibility of thought and action. You will be able to exercise your talents: empathy, curiosity, research, judgment, insight, creativity, imagination, and persistence.

To make this five-step process complete, more effective, and easier to use, three elements that will help you channel and control your thinking are presented in the next chapter.

8

Controlling the Persuasion Process

The five steps presented so far represent the heart of the persuasion process. You establish someone's needs, propose a means of filling those needs, tell how the plan works, explain its benefits, and ask for the order. This is straightforward and might seem to be enough to go on. Unfortunately, it is not.

Ongoing experience with thousands of people in our seminar-workshops shows that as people build their proposals, they need a method to guide and control the thinking process behind the proposal, as well as some way to analyze the logic of the various steps in relation to the others. Needlessly complicating? No! Actually, the controls end up by simplifying the process. You would be astonished at how many otherwise intelligent people fail to get firm control of the persuasion process in the beginning and have no way of checking and analyzing their efforts during or on completion of their work. These people consistently fail at persuasion tasks. Worse, they seldom figure out where and why they went wrong.

Controlling the Process With Three Added Steps

To help you avoid such debacles, let's add three steps to the five you already learned. With them we will pull the process together into one neat, integrated tool. The three added steps are AUDIENCE DEFINITION, YOUR OBJECTIVE, and NEEDS AGREEMENT.

These are controls to help keep your thinking on track. They also provide a means of helping you to align and analyze the logic of your proposals *before* you present them. Here is where they fit:

1. **AUDIENCE DEFINITION**
2. **YOUR OBJECTIVE**
3. NEEDS
4. **NEEDS AGREEMENT** (Yes/No)
5. PLAN
6. HOW-IT-WORKS
7. RESULTS
8. NEXT STEP

Audience Definition

This first step, AUDIENCE DEFINITION, seems so obvious that it should go without saying. Unfortunately, inexperienced people do not devote sufficient attention to their target. Many also overlook the *secondary audience*—people who are influential in the decision process but who are not addressed directly. Thus, the sources of many major problems with persuasive messages are there at the beginning. Either the originator does not have the audience in sharp focus, or the objective has not been properly set and clearly defined. Sometimes both steps are flawed. You need to know your audience, exactly *who* you are addressing. And you need to have a solid objective, one that says exactly *what* you expect to accomplish with the proposal you plan to develop. This may seem like an elaboration of the obvious, but it is not.

The WHO: Is the person (or group) you are addressing empowered to act on the proposal you are developing? Does that person have the authority, the influence, the right, the money, the budget, or whatever is required to authorize or take the action you propose? If not, stop until you have found the audience who can. This is unequivocal. There is no sense in proposing something to someone who does not have the power to act. If you wish to propose marriage, whom would you ask?

When you have targeted your audience, and you think you

know who has the power of decision, don't be too sure. How well do you know this person? Is this person a loner, an independent decision maker, or will you be put off while he or she turns to someone else for advice, guidance, and/or permission? Do you know if there are any other important people in the background who could influence the decision? If so, how do these people relate to and influence the decision-making process of your prime audience?

For example, are you automatically addressing your boss's boss when you address your boss? When you make a proposal to a person in a small business, are you also addressing that person's banker, lawyer, or CPA? Suppose you wish to persuade me to make a business investment. Must you consider the influence of my wife or financial adviser as part of the audience, or would you offend me if you suggested that? Think about the people, other than the person(s) addressed directly, who might be shown a proposal you wrote. Suppose your audience is a group. Are the interests and needs of all its members the same, or must you recognize and deal with discrete segments that have different interests and needs?

How much do you really need to know about your audience? Sometimes you need to know a lot. A long-term, steady customer can be an ongoing study. In others cases, knowing next to nothing may be enough. Only you can decide the extent of the research required. On the one hand, you don't necessarily have to build a dossier on the person you wish to persuade. On the other, you can never know too much. Bear in mind that your business is persuasion, and you want to cut off your research as soon as you have enough to go on. Whatever you learn about your audience, just be sure that that person has the power to accept your proposal.

The Objective

The second of the three added steps is YOUR OBJECTIVE. It is a carefully crafted statement, *written by you in no more than fifty words*. It says exactly what you intend to accomplish with this particular proposal. It is your message to you. It provides you with direction. It is not to form part of the message your audience will get because *your* needs are embodied here. Your objective will have a direct influence on two other steps in the process, namely, PLAN and NEXT STEP.

Without a well-thought-out objective, any proposal is most likely to be out of control from the beginning. With one, you are likely to move through your thinking process with very little difficulty. Experience also shows that if you need more than fifty words to write an objective for a proposal, you probably don't yet really know what you are trying to do. More thinking is in order.

Let me emphasize, your objective defines the action you want to get with *this* proposal *and nothing more.* For example, if you wish to sell someone a car, you can simply say that, if that really is all you want to do with the proposal. Most car salespersons would include the price, the profit, and other conditions of sale they needed to meet. The objective might be to sell the red, belch-fire coupé today for not less than $22,595 to Miss Jones. Maybe the objective is to clear the way for the new models by selling off this last car. Or it might be to qualify for a special bonus.

Most of us, when developing objectives, have a tendency to become preoccupied by the immediate and to forget to *think beyond the thing itself.* Take Jim Weston's experience, for example.

Ends vs. Means

As one of our seminar-workshop participants, Weston was a high-ranking official in a large manufacturing plant. He was in charge of a major segment of this plant.

When Weston presented his proposal to the workshop group, he said his objective was to persuade his boss to approve the construction of a huge and very expensive elevator (the thing) to run between the first and second floors of the plant. Another participant asked Weston how he would use the elevator. Weston said he planned to move both people and product faster, safer, and cheaper. Another participant suggested that the result—moving people and product faster, more safely and cheaply—was the real objective and not the elevator per se.

At first Weston disagreed. He repeated, with emphasis, that

he wanted the elevator, period. Finally, someone asked him if he would still want the elevator if he could accomplish the same task by another means, such as with a magic wand, an escalator, or a sky hook. Eureka! Weston beamed as if he himself had thought beyond the thing itself. He saw that he could view his objective differently, allowing the elevator to become the means instead of the end. The result was that he gained better control of his thought processes as he developed his proposal.

Weston might have gone even further. Suppose that moving people and product in a faster, safer, and cheaper way would result in breaking a costly bottleneck, one that would reduce production costs. Then Jim Weston might have written his objective as follows: *To get approval for a plan to reduce production costs by 0.5 percent and increase safety by moving people and product between the first and second floors with a new elevator* (30 words).

Thinking beyond the thing itself is good practice and should be done routinely. As you write your objectives, ask yourself some questions: What will this do for me? Is this all I want out of my proposal? Am I defining the end I want or just the means? Jim Weston really did not want an elevator for its own sake; he did not even want to move people and product faster. Rather, when boiled down, his real objective was to reduce costs and increase safety.

Needs Agreement

The third step is NEEDS AGREEMENT. This is simply a reminding yes-or-no question. It asks whether or not you have confirmed that your prospect's needs are as you believe they are. If the answer is no and you have access to your prospect, ask. There are many times, however, when you can't make personal contact with your prospect. Therefore, you will go on with the development of your proposal using assumed needs. All you can do in situations like this is to make your best guess. Risky? Yes, but it's often unavoidable.

This is what advertisers do every day. They assume that a percentage of their readers, listeners, or viewers have certain needs. They build their advertisements on this assumption, hoping that the venture will pay off. You can do the same thing with any proposal. Just recognize the risk. John Wanamaker, the onetime tycoon of retailing, was credited with saying that only half his advertising paid off. Unfortunately, he could not tell which half would pay until after he had run all the advertising.

Debugging Your Proposals

As you go on creating proposals, inevitably you will struggle with one that just won't come together. Worse, you will somehow fail to identify the flaws, let alone correct them. Take heart. This happens to everyone. Either concentrated thinking or personal bias can cause a loss of perspective.

You may be too close to your project and need to step back to take a fresh look. This is where a special debugging tool fits in. We call it the Structure and Alignment Chart (see Figure 8-1). With it, you can isolate and examine the individual structural parts of your proposal and see how they relate to each other. This technique will make it easier for you to analyze your own work objectively. By examining structural parts, you will cut through the detail, view the logic and flow of your ideas in a new light, find the problems, and correct them.

You will like the Structure and Alignment Chart. It is easy to use because it summarizes *The Anatomy of Persuasion* process on a single page. All you need do is check three alignments. With this technique you can identify, diagnose, and fix flaws *before* your presentation. Furthermore, you can quickly refresh your skill at any time by looking at this chart. So, keep it handy; even a lifetime skill needs an occasional tune-up.

First Alignment

The reasoning here says that your OBJECTIVE states what you want to accomplish with this proposal. The PLAN, derived directly from your OBJECTIVE, tells what you propose that your audience do to satisfy the needs established. And your NEXT STEP asks the audience to take the specific action requested in the plan. There must be a logical flow of thought from the objective through the plan and on to the next step. This is absolutely criti-

Figure 8-1. Structure and Alignment Chart.

Rules of Construction

(1) Write your OBJECTIVE in 50 words or less. Derive your statements of PLAN and NEXT STEP from your OBJECTIVE. You should have a logical flow of thought from OBJECTIVE through PLAN to NEXT STEP.

(2) The NEEDS of your audience should be completely developed and the RESULTS should translate the NEEDS into appropriate BENE-FITS. Be sure to check the sequence.

(3) Your HOW-IT-WORKS should tell your audience only what it needs to know in principle to understand how your PLAN will be carried out.

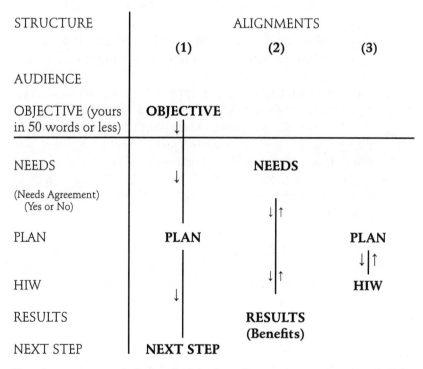

To analyze your proposal, check each of the three alignments separately against the Rules of Construction. When each alignment meets its rule, chances are that the whole proposal will work well when assembled.

cal. Proposals that do not have this logical flow are structurally weak and are likely to fail.

For a simple example, let's say that your OBJECTIVE is to sell your old car to your pal Charlie instead of trading it on a new car. After you have covered Charlie's NEEDS, your PLAN statement is quite simple. You say, "Charlie, to satisfy your needs, I propose that you buy my car." This follows logically from your OBJECTIVE. Then, after covering the HIW and RESULTS (benefits) with Charlie, you go on with your NEXT STEP by asking Charlie for the order. You say, "How about it, Charlie, is it a deal?"

This is a simple and straightforward sequence, but there is a snag at this point for many people. They don't want to ask for the order or the action. This snag is as common as stage fright. People fear rejection or failure or disappointment. This is where you must bite the bullet and ask for what you want.

Let's examine the first alignment in Jim Weston's proposal (the revised, logical version) to his boss concerning the elevator:

- Weston's OBJECTIVE: To get approval of a plan to reduce production costs by 0.5 percent and increase safety by moving people and product between the first and second floors via a new elevator *(a clear statement of what Jim wants to accomplish with this proposal)*.
- His PLAN: Authorize a project to install an elevator *(a clear statement, derived from the OBJECTIVE, of what Weston proposes his boss do to satisfy his needs to reduce costs and safety hazards)*.
- Weston's NEXT STEP: Please sign this work authorization so that the project can be started immediately and be completed and operating within ninety days *(a request for the action set forth in the PLAN by a specific time)*.

Failure to achieve a logical flow of thought from OBJECTIVE through PLAN and on to NEXT STEP is a common fault. Although Weston did a good job with his actual proposal, he could have set himself up for failure with just one slip. Let's say that he decided to put this proposal in written form and to send it to his boss. The structure of the proposal remains the same except when Weston changes the NEXT STEP. He asks for a meeting to discuss the idea instead of asking the plant manager to sign a work authorization. This flaws his logic because this step does not ask for the action proposed in the PLAN that was derived from his OBJECTIVE. Weston's objective was to get approval for a project, not to have a meeting. If he had wanted a meeting, his OBJECTIVE should have stated as much. This would have been a completely different proposal. But, since a meeting was not what Jim wanted, he created a misalignment by suggesting one. He did not ask for specific action by a specific time. This represents a major fault in his thinking and in his proposal—an all-too-common fault in many proposals. If you don't ask for specific action by a specific time, you are likely not to get it.

There are other ways to flaw the First Alignment. For example, if your PLAN statement is not derived from your OBJECTIVE, you will have trouble throughout the effort. Your proposal simply will not jell. If your OBJECTIVE is incorrect or merely short-sighted, as was Weston's before he revised it, you will have problems. By checking the First Alignment, your structural shortfalls will become obvious and usually correctable.

Second Alignment

This aligns and connects NEEDS and RESULTS (benefits). Remember, this refers to the needs of your audience, not to your own needs. More than that, it involves needs as perceived by your audience, not your idea of what they might be.

Once you have established the NEEDS your audience has, you have a firm foundation. Then, after you present the PLAN to satisfy the prospect's needs and explain how the plan works (HIW), you must connect the outcome, or RESULTS, with the NEEDS. This is vitally important because it presents the benefits that the audience will get and shows how these fill each need included in the proposal. This connection must be firm and positive. This is not casual; it is calculated. As with a picture puzzle, when you put these key pieces in place, your proposal will come alive. Your audience will visualize, feel, and understand exactly what the benefits are and exactly how these will satisfy the needs discussed.

The essential thing about the Second Alignment is that the

NEEDS of your audience be translated into the RESULTS, or benefits. This is to be the payoff for your audience. Therefore, the tie-in between each NEED and each RESULT (benefit) must be absolutely clear. We buy ideas, products, and services not because of what these things *are* but because of what these things *do* for us. For every need there must be a fulfilling benefit.

One way to improve your communication of NEEDS and RESULTS is to match and align them in sequence. (The line numbers on the Outline Guide will help you.) As you present and get agreement on a series of needs, you create a mind-set. Your audience will process and relate the information about the benefits more easily if you present them in the same order in which you presented the needs. This way your message meshes with the mind-set you created.

Third Alignment

This aligns the PLAN and HOW-IT-WORKS (HIW). The HIW part tells the audience, in principle, how the plan will be carried out. The plan is what the seller proposes the buyer do to satisfy his or her needs. HOW-IT-WORKS is an explanation of the plan in sufficient detail to provide the prospect with an understanding in principle of how the plan will be carried out. Please note that the HIW part does not call for a detailed elaboration. You must provide only the essential information. Getting involved in detail here can be diverting and can disrupt the flow of your proposal on to its most important part—the RESULTS (benefits).

Sometimes deciding what is essential for an understanding in principle can involve a delicate balance. For example, if you were selling me a car and you mentioned the horsepower of the engine, I would want to know about the torque—the number of foot pounds, where the peak is, and so on. I have queried dozens of car salesmen regarding how many people ask about engine torque. They all tell me that this is a real "oddball" question. Not more than one in 200 prospects asks about it. This says that if you are selling cars, don't volunteer information about torque. Even though it is one of the most important features affecting the performance of any car, almost no one cares. So knowing your audience will help. Asking others what they would need to know in order to grasp the plan in principle will help. Wise men tell us, "The Devil is in the details." People with skill and experience in the persuasion process tell us, "You better believe it."

In Jim Weston's proposal, the PLAN was: *I propose that you approve the construction of a special elevator.* If you were Weston's boss, you might want to know something about how the elevator would change the work flow; how much it would cost; who would build or install it; how long the project would take; if there were any ramifications such as safety, insurance, or union problems; and whether area superintendents and first-line supervisors had seen and endorsed the idea. Jim could tick those off quickly without tangling himself in detail.

Think in terms of the familiar questions taught in journalism courses: who, when, where, why, how, how much, and how long. Then, in the interests of brevity, provide only the minimum information needed. Keep the rest of the detail in your head and be ready to answer questions should they develop. In short: Overkill your preparation, and underkill your proposal; make it concise, brief, and keep the Devil at bay.

Summary

To summarize, there are three steps to control the persuasion process: AUDIENCE, OBJECTIVE, and NEEDS AGREEMENT. And there is a means to judge the logical relationship of the parts in any given proposal with the three alignments. You will find, as you practice developing proposals, that these elements will blend to form a dependable method of creating, presenting, and analyzing any persuasive message that you create or that may come to your attention.

You may want to use the Structure and Alignment Chart as a routine procedure each time you finish a proposal, just as aviators use checkoff lists before takeoff. Many a butt has been preserved intact by such prudence. There is a bonus benefit here. The use of the Structure and Alignment Chart can help you neutralize your own worst enemy. This is your personal bias, especially the kind that is enhanced by the unbridled enthusiasm you may generate from time to time.

How many times have you come up with an absolutely "brilliant" idea that bombed miserably? Such debacles happen to all of us. Our personal biases blind us to reality. We occasionally overlook the fact that some of our most cherished ideas really are poor, fallacious, unworkable, and absolutely unacceptable to others. When we do that, we set ourselves up as sure losers. There is a real bonus benefit in your ability to view your idea as others may see it. To do this, *examine your Second Alignment carefully.* Recheck to be sure your proposal really fills your audience's needs. If it does not, quit now. Egg on your face will not improve your image.

Practice is essential to building your skill. Obviously, preparing proposals of your own is the best way. Between times there is another way, a fun way, to practice this thinking process. You can analyze advertisements you see in the normal course of your reading. You will recognize some ads as terrible, a gross waste of money, even though they were prepared with good intentions by professional advertising people. Many others are mediocre at best. Some rank as acceptable. A very few are great.

What you know already about the persuasion process qualifies you to judge advertising with expertise. Just follow the thinking process you are learning, and you can analyze advertising and rate it with confidence and reason. For the fun of it, imagine you are the person who approves the advertising your company runs. Your advertising manager presents an ad. You read it carefully and then ask the following questions:

1. AUDIENCE: Who do we intend to reach?
2. OBJECTIVE: What, exactly, are we trying to accomplish with this ad? (Remember, a fifty-word statement is the maximum explanation needed. If your advertising manager tries to give you a speech, beware.)
3. NEEDS: Has this ad really established the needs of our audience?
4. PLAN and HIW: Is what we propose as a means of satisfying the established needs clear and understandable?
5. RESULTS: Does this ad express and connect the benefits

of our proposal with the needs we believe our audience has?

6. NEXT STEP: Does this ad make it as easy as possible for our audience to take specific action by a specific time?
7. How will we measure the results of this ad to help us decide whether it paid us to run it?

9

Features, Functions, and Benefits

When creating *The Anatomy of Persuasion* seminar-workshop, I asked for ideas and suggestions from friends and acquaintances who had been active and successful in the training business. One such person was an outstanding director of training I had known for many years. His effective and innovative programs, especially in sales and marketing, had earned him an enviable reputation. He asked me if I planned to include the subject of features and benefits. I told him that I did not, because although I knew the vital role this concept plays in the persuasion process, I believed that most of the people we expected to train already knew enough to make its inclusion seem repetitive and boring.

He told me point-blank that I was absolutely, unequivocally, completely, and totally wrong. Bitter experience had taught him that most people do not know the important differences between a feature and a benefit. He said that not one person in ten can define either one, let alone translate a feature and express it as a benefit. He emphasized this by saying that most people do not even understand the important role a knowledge of features and benefits plays in their personal ability to persuade others. Before I could take a breath, he went on to advise me to include the subject, and he also provided several suggestions about how to do it.

Despite my reluctance to accept his idea, I decided to follow his suggestion just on the chance that he was right. Later, and still unconvinced, I faced my first audience of ten managers of a medium-size company with trepidation. Most of these people had come up through sales. They should have had a solid knowledge of features and benefits. Therefore, I was expecting at best a ho-hum reaction, if not an outright negative one. To my astonishment, the response was favorable. They admitted that they really had not understood the subject and considered the information useful and appropriate. Since then, we have kept features and benefits in every seminar. Over the years, only a few people have said that they considered it repetitive. So, if you are well informed on the subject, please skip to the next chapter.

Features vs. Benefits

We buy ideas, products, and services not because of what these things *are* but because of what these things *do*. When we *define* a feature and a benefit, we say a feature is the thing. That thing can be anything—a pencil, a proposed merger, a vacation, a reorganization plan, a bank account, ownership of a car, a bill in Congress. You name the thing, and that is the feature. A benefit is what the feature does for you. For example, consider the benefits of a pencil. It makes effective communication possible. It improves your memory and efficiency. You make shopping lists to recall exactly what items you want, get them, and complete the task without forgetting anything or wasting time trying to remember.

When we buy a coffeemaker, we are really buying thousands of gallons of hot coffee. The coffee is the feature. What it does for us is the benefit, like the pure joy of drinking freshly brewed coffee when and where we want it. To some the aroma alone signals the start of a fresh new day, promising something pleasant, an inner comfort, a feeling of opportunity or well-being. The benefit may be the "lift," from sleepiness to full functioning, we get from the brew itself. To others coffee taken after dinner may represent the pleasure of group conviviality, the warmth and security of friends and fellowship. Whatever, for most people, benefits are what we want when we buy a thing called a coffeemaker—or anything else.

What's in a Screwdriver?

Your ability to *translate* a feature (a thing) into a benefit (what the thing does) is an indispensable skill in the art of persuasion. Let's practice this ability on a not-so-common screwdriver. Look at it and name several of its features (see Figure 9-1). You may come up with this short list:

Features

- Plastic handle
- Square shank
- Craftsman brand name

Then, try translating each feature into a benefit and list them, too:

Features	*Benefits*
Plastic handle	Electric insulation
Square shank	More twisting power
Craftsman brand name	Lifetime guarantee

Notice that the square shank will accept a wrench. This allows the user to apply far more twisting power (torque) than could be achieved were the shank round like most screwdrivers.

Sears offers a lifetime guarantee for their Craftsman line of hand tools. If you are ever not satisfied with your Craftsman hand tool, you may take it to any Sears store for replacement without charge. Most people we have met know about the Sears guarantee and automatically make the translation from feature (Craftsman) to benefit (lifetime guarantee).

Figure 9-1. Sears's Craftsman square-shank screwdriver.

As you study the features/benefits list, you may not notice that these so-called benefits are really only intermediate stopping points in the translation of a feature to a benefit. They are actually *functions*. To illustrate the point, ask yourself what benefit you get from having a screwdriver with an insulated handle. What does it do for you? Answer: It prevents electric shocks (function). And what good is that? Answer: You avoid serious injury or death (benefit). Thus, the arrangement is altered by adding functions in between features and benefits. This forces you to project your thinking onward to an ultimate expression of the benefit for any given feature.

Features	Functions	Benefits
Plastic handle	Electric insulation	Avoids injury/ death
Square shank	More twisting power	Does tougher jobs
Craftsman brand name	Lifetime guarantee	Low cost/long run

The idea is to continue your search for however long it takes you to find the expression of ultimate benefit. What does a lifetime guarantee do for you? Perhaps it says that in the long run this screwdriver will cost less than others do because it will never be allowed to wear out (Sears offers a free replacement if it is damaged).

When translating features to benefits, there are two cautions. Most times *you* should make the translation for your audience so that you can control the thinking process. And you should be sure that the ultimate benefit you describe ties directly into an established need. For instance, with the screwdriver, the square shank is translated into *Does tougher jobs*. The idea here is that with a wrench applied to the square shaft, users can remove stubborn screws that otherwise they could not budge. It's a nice idea and an obvious benefit for some people. But if you allow your audience to make the translation, the situation can sometimes get out of control.

Suppose I am a screwdriver salesman using this benefit to sell my square-shank screwdrivers to a service manager of a large auto repair garage for use by his mechanics when they have stubborn screws to remove. I assume the need, because I have sold a lot of square-shank screwdrivers to similar garages for just this purpose. After showing the screwdriver to the service manager, I controlled the translation from feature to benefit by pointing out that, with a wrench attached, his mechanics could remove stubborn screws more easily (feature).

Before I could get to the benefit (completes tough jobs faster), however, the service manager exploded. He told me to hide the screwdriver instantly and not let any of his mechanics see it. "Never bring one in again with a square shank," he insisted. When asked why, the service manager said that if his stupid mechanics had square-shank screwdrivers to loosen screws, they would also use these screwdrivers to tighten screws. They would overdo everything, strip threads, and wind up doing costly damage instead of becoming more efficient at tough jobs, as I proposed. A lesson learned, I hope!

To Translate or Not to Translate

You can't be sure that your audiences will make the translation from feature to benefit in every situation unless you do it for them. All of us, when making buying decisions, are primarily concerned with what's in it for us. We are on the lookout for benefits. Bear in mind, however, a benefit can also be viewed negatively, as the screwdriver's effectiveness was by the service manager.

This may seem like a contradiction, but there are times when you should not make the translation for your audience. When the translation is obvious or when the prospect has already made it himself, you are advised to leave well enough alone. The "lift" (feature) you get from the coffee may be enough. Most people have made that translation and don't need us to tell them what waking up feels like. And how do you translate the benefit of a cosmetic product to a particular individual? Are you selling healthy skin or dreams of romance? Be careful here. Take into consideration the age, personality, and intelligence of your audience before you pitch the benefit. In general, make the translation for your audience, but remember that there are always exceptions. However it is, you are in charge of making the call.

Looking for the Ultimate Benefit

But before you make the call, think it through in advance and guide the process. To do this, keep asking and answering the question "So what?" The objective always is to find the ultimate benefit for your particular audience. For example, let's assume that the product is a computer. So what? Our computer has a 1,000 gigabyte hard disk. So what? So you can store all your files in your computer. So what? So you don't have to clutter up your office with thousands of paper files. So what? So you can find information you need when you need it. So what? So you can work faster, better, more efficiently. Bingo!

This process goes on until you arrive at the ultimate benefit. This is the highest and most persuasive truth that fills an actual need and moves your audience to accept your proposal. Consider an electronic calculator (feature). So what? It helps you do your income tax return. So what? It speeds up the process. So what? You eliminate arithmetic errors. So what? You reduce the risk of an IRS audit. Bingo!

While we're at it, let's develop the ultimate benefit of the calculator when your checkbook needs attention. The calculator helps you get it right the first time. So what? It saves you aggravation. So what! It helps you avoid a possible overdraft penalty. Bingo again.

Get in the habit of thinking in terms of the benefits your product, service, or idea will bring to the people who might use it.

One of our seminar participants, an engineer in a large chemical manufacturing company, told us he had invented a device that would predict the failure of pressure-relief valves. Such valves are used to prevent the buildup of excessive pressure in tanks and boilers in chemical manufacturing processes. When a pressure-relief valve fails, an explosive blowout can occur and cause a costly shutdown and sometimes serious injury to plant personnel. During the past four years, however, this engineer had been unable to convince manufacturing people in his company to use this device even though the company had over 100,000 such valves in operation, and he had a four-year, successful demonstration at one plant. All the plant people he had contacted told him that top management said no money would be spent on new equipment during these tight economic times, period.

He went on to tell us how his device worked. He had figured out that when these valves were approaching failure, they would start to vibrate. You could not detect this vibration with eye or ear, but he could detect it by attaching a small, inexpensive electronic patch. This patch would send out a signal to warn of impending danger. With advance knowledge, the valve could be conveniently replaced before failure.

We said, "So what?"

At first the man was insulted and angry. He told us we were reacting just like the many plant people he had talked with. We responded by telling him that the benefits of his device were not self-evident. He was like the lonely man with the better mousetrap. After he had explained more about his device's features and benefits, we said "So what" again.

This time he caught on. He said, "So plant people don't have to do preventive maintenance on these valves anymore." So what? "They won't need to replace each valve every so often regardless of its condition." So what? "You replace only the valves that are about to fail." So what? "You cut maintenance costs, because you don't replace a lot of expensive valves that are still in good working order" (benefit). So what? "You eliminate costly shutdowns due to pressure-relief valve failure" (benefit). So what? "You eliminate a potential safety hazard" (benefit). By now, in spite of the third-degree treatment, he was smiling. He could smell success.

We suggested that he keep thinking and talking this way, that he develop numbers on the cost savings and then find plant managers whose needs were to cut overall costs and increase safety. This engineer completed the seminar-workshop with an outstanding proposal along these lines. We checked back with him three months later to find him on cloud nine.

"Your training worked like magic," he said. "I have installed my device on 2,000 valves so far and I have a large backlog of orders with more coming in every day." Bingo! Bingo! Bingo!

What's in a Brand Name?

Some features translate automatically and go pretty much in a predictable way. Consider the brand name Maytag as a feature. The owners of that name have worked hard to make it mean quality, reliability, high value-in-use, freedom from worry about breakdowns and costly repairs, and so on. For most people, this translation from feature to benefit travels in a straight line to exactly where the Maytag people want it—a brand name that automatically and predictably translates to specific benefits that prospective customers value and for which some people are willing to pay a premium price.

Other brand names do not always behave like this. The Mercedes name gets different translations from different people. If you ask John why he bought a Mercedes, you will hear about quality of workmanship, excellence of engineering, outstanding safety, high retained value, and so forth. If you ask a neighbor why John bought a Mercedes, you might hear that John does not really care about the workmanship. Nor would he recognize good engineering if he fell over it, because John's mechanical aptitude is near zero. John is feeding his ego. He wants to convince his world that he has arrived. The neighbor also notes ostentation. John parks his old car in the closed garage out of sight. The Mercedes is always parked outside in plain view.

Before we make too much fun of John's behavior, remember that most of us have a need for a personal identity, for a statement, if you please. John is making his in his way. Mary, having bought a Mercedes like John's, is making her statement in her way. A young, up-and-coming local attorney, Mary speaks of her Mercedes rather bluntly:

> I don't care about all that engineering stuff. I drive these ridiculously expensive wheels not because someone says

it's a good car or because I want to impress my friends and neighbors. I use this car purely as an advertisement to remind prospective clients that I am a young, successful, energetic lawyer, and that when they need legal help, they should call me. If I couldn't get a tax write-off on a car, I'd drive a cheaper one and get my message out some other way.

Summary

In sum, a feature is the thing. A benefit is what that thing does for you. So, as you construct a proposal, you develop the NEEDS of your audience. As you do this, you think in terms of the NEEDS and how they are perceived. This perception may be expressed as a feature or it may come out as a benefit. You must identify the benefit that fills the need as your audience perceives it.

You now know the basics of the persuasion process. You know the thinking process we all use when we make a buying decision, and you have learned a thinking process to mesh with that. Now you are ready to practice. The next chapter will not only introduce you to a winning proposal; it will also take you behind the scenes to reveal the exact details of its construction. This particular proposal served as a pattern for proposals that helped a small business become very successful.

10

Setting Your Objective

The keystone of a successful proposal is its OBJECTIVE. Your ability to set clear, concise, unambiguous objectives for your proposals is essential. The objective for any proposal will influence all the other parts. This chapter presents a few suggestions on setting objectives that will help you aim your proposals and keep them on target.

Your OBJECTIVE defines the purpose of your proposal. It governs the flow of your ideas and your logic throughout the persuasion process. It is the foundation of your proposal. It is *you* telling *you* what *you* want to accomplish with this proposal *and nothing more.*

Note that the word *you* appears three times in the last sentence. Could anything be more emphatic? The objective for your proposal embodies your needs. It describes your payoff. Although it is an essential part of the structure of your proposal, it does not appear in the actual communication you present to your audience because your objective is your private business, for your eyes only.

Your objective describes *what* you want to accomplish. It describes the outcome, the result. It does not describe the how, the process, the means, or the procedure for achieving the result. Navigators do not plot courses until they have decided on a destination. Builders do not select materials until they have studied a blueprint. So before you propose anything, take the time to create a solid objective.

If you get your objective right in the beginning, I guarantee that you will stay on track with your proposal. You will be organized; you will have defined the result you seek. You will maintain both focus and perspective throughout the experience of creating and delivering your proposal. No matter what the outcome, success or failure, you will understand both the process and the result.

If you get your objective wrong, I guarantee that you will be disorganized from beginning to end. You will become frustrated. You will spin your wheels and increase your probability of failure. If you learn anything, it should be what you have read so far in this chapter, namely, that it is mandatory to get your objective right in the first place. If you do happen to succeed with an ill-conceived objective, it will only be by pure chance.

Take careful aim. Successful persuasion requires precise, short-term thinking. This is not to say that you should be a shortsighted person or that you should not have vision and long-term planning skills. It is to say that there are times when you move from strategic to tactical thinking and action. You deal with the "now" because that is where the action is as of right now. Therefore, please keep in mind that your objective is for this proposal only.

Suppose you say that your objective is to become a long-term supplier to the Blank Corporation. "Long-term" to you means a five-year relationship. Is the first step to establish a five-year contract? If so, okay. But, most likely, there are some essential steps in between. If you are to become a regular, long-term supplier to the Blank Corporation, you may need a number of proposals to achieve that. Meantime, your immediate objective may be to get a six-month contract as a preliminary to the longer-term goal. If so, that may be the objective for this proposal, because this is what you must do next. Think about your five-year proposal later. By that time, the five-year proposal will be "this" proposal, and you will be right back thinking of the "now" again.

To develop an objective for a proposal, think in terms of your purpose—*what* you want to do. When your ideas begin to flow, get them on paper fast. Capitalize on your output. Don't stop to organize. Use key words; use phrases instead of sentences. Only after the flow stops should you try to distill your notes into your finished, written objective of not more than fifty words. After you have a first draft on paper, let it rest for a while.

After the rest, analyze your work again in terms of the specific action you wish to get with this proposal. Start by substituting "tight" words for "loose" words. "Loose" words can be interpreted or misinterpreted in many ways. "Tight" words are specific in their meaning and denote definitive action or behavior. Here are a few examples:

Loose Words	Tight Words
know	recall, recite, write, identify
understand	define, demonstrate, show, tell
appreciate	describe, compare, rate, increase
value	price, appraise, reckon, quantify

Next, substitute "tight" ideas for "loose" ideas. Check for abstract, indefinite, intangible, indefinable, and fuzzy expressions. If your first efforts read like certain lofty goal and mission statements you may have seen, watch out. Some of these statements are as unworthy as a leaky boat in a heavy sea. For example:

- Become more customer-oriented.
- Improve community relations.
- Enhance our social conscience.
- Develop a sense of community spirit.
- Have a better understanding of . . .
- Influence professional ethics in a positive manner.
- Develop a more favorable attitude.
- Take greater pride in our work.
- Know our competition . . . customer . . . market.
- Create value and build trust.
- Increase the self-confidence of . . .

Try the last fuzzy, for example. Suppose our objective is to increase the self-confidence of our plant foremen. Since we can't measure self-confidence, let's ask our favorite question, "So what?" So, if these people increased their self-confidence, what behavioral change might we notice? They might speak up and share more of their first-line knowledge and experience with management on a regular basis. So what? Their knowledge and hands-on production experience might help us cut costs, save time, or improve quality. So what? We might be able to persuade each foreman to make weekly presentations to management covering raw materials, production, quality, costs, personnel, safety, plus ideas for improvement. Wait a minute! That sounds more like a *how.* We need a *what.* One more "so what" gets us to the final cut, and that gives us an acceptable *what* and the objective emerges:

To persuade our foremen to increase their participation with management in the operation of the plant.

Note: We also carved out the *how* in the process (weekly presentations to management), which we can save for use in the PLAN part of our actual proposal.

The message here is that when you prepare an objective for your proposal, you should define the undefined, jell the intangible, and solidify the abstract. If you do not identify the *what,* you will not be able to decide *how* you want to do it. Worse, if you cannot tell the difference between a *what* and a *how,* you might get them reversed. That is a "not good" situation that some would describe with the old cliché about putting the cart before the horse. An objective that is bassackwards will help you create a proposal that has the same characteristics. Such proposals not only fail; they also stain the presenter's image—a much deserved but avoidable outcome.

As you work on your objective, please bear in mind that fifty words are almost always more than enough to do the job. Objectives of more than fifty words usually lack the clarity essential to describe the outcome in a crisp, unequivocal manner.

Once you have an objective on paper, test it to determine whether you are clearly focused on the *what* rather than on the *how.* You can do this with a little exercise we call *thinking beyond the thing itself.* Use the "so what" question again. Let's go back to Jim Weston, the manufacturing official who wanted to get a project approved to build an expensive elevator. If we ask "so what?" we are seeking the purpose of the elevator, namely *what* it will do. Answer: The elevator will move people and product faster, safer, and cheaper. So what? That will save time, reduce costs, and prevent accidents. Finally, after enough "so what" questions, the objective becomes clear.

If you recall, Weston did not at first separate his *what* from his *how* (elevator). He was satisfied that his objective was to get an elevator. Therefore, he defined a *how* rather than a *what*. Later, after a few "so whats," he developed a clear definition of the *what* and put that first. Then he subordinated the elevator to the PLAN part of his proposal as he realized that what he wanted was to reduce costs and improve safety. That got Weston to the useful, workable objective you will remember from Chapter 8:

To get approval for a plan to reduce production costs by 0.5 percent and increase safety in the movement of people and product between the first and second floors (28 words).

Make your objective measurable. Ask yourself what indicators you will see when you have achieved your objective. If you can measure performance or behavior or outcome in some definitive manner, your objective probably is as solid as you can make it.

In Jim Weston's case, he knows that a 0.5 percent reduction in production costs is $10,000 per month. He knows the number of personal injuries that have occurred in previous years, so he knows how to measure future safety performance if his proposal is approved and the elevator is put in service.

Let's convert a few abstract objectives to concrete statements that can be measured.

- *Abstract Objective:* To get our service people to improve their understanding of our customers' needs.
- *Concrete Objective:* To get each service person to name the five most important needs of each customer with whom he/she deals.

- *Abstract Objective:* To develop a better working relationship between our truck drivers and our customers' shipping personnel.

- *Concrete Objective:* To improve the on-time arrivals of our trucks at customers' locations from 75 percent to 95 percent.

- *Abstract Objective:* To teach our employees to be more courteous to patients.
- *Concrete Objective:* To teach our employees how to remember patients' names and titles and the proper etiquette for using them.

Look before you leap. There are times when our impatience (or some false sense of urgency) sweeps us into an action before we have thought through and defined our exact purpose. Because this is a mistake most of us make sooner or later, a reminder might help. Ask yourself if you really have enough information about the situation to be even considering a proposal of any kind. Impulsive reactions usually net unwanted setbacks of one kind or another.

Once upon a time the president of a large corporation was having an informal lunch with two of his vice presidents, Stan and Ed. The conversation meandered through yesterday's sports, touched on a political scandal, and lulled into interest rates. At the lull, the president asked if either VP knew anything about the economy in Wheeling, West Virginia. Neither did, but Stan, preempting Ed, said he would check. Stan believed this was a sign of something big, confidential, and important. Ed tried unsuccessfully to dissuade Stan from proposing a quick but expensive ($10,000) study to answer the question about Wheeling until they knew more about what their boss had in mind. Stan proposed the study anyway. The president gave Stan a quick turndown. He explained in a curt tone that his question about Wheeling was prompted by his next-door neighbor. It seems the neighbor's daughter was thinking of going to college in Wheeling and wondered whether she would have half a chance of finding a part-time job there. Stan wondered whether this incident would come up as a rebuke in his next performance review. It did! Ed chuckles quietly every time he thinks of the incident.

In summary, when you have prepared an objective for your

proposal, before you do anything else take a last look to be sure it describes the action you wish to get in clear, definitive language that defies misinterpretation. And, oh yes, no more than fifty words, please.

11

Using the Tools

All the parts will come together for you in this chapter. You will see a complete proposal done in *The Anatomy of Persuasion* style. It is an actual proposal, and it was successful. The writer, Mary Davis, using only one page, persuaded a prospective buyer of an old, rundown apartment building to hire her to coordinate the rehabilitation of the property. You will also go behind the scenes to see how Mary constructed her proposal using the Outline Guide (see Appendix III). This is a one-page form, complete with easy-to-read instructions, to help guide your thinking as you prepare your own proposals. The Outline Guide will serve as your basic, lifetime tool whenever you wish to construct *any* communication intended to persuade others.

Learning the Hard Way

Background: Mary launched her career with what she had learned as a participant in one of our first seminar-workshops. She was exceptionally talented at what she did for herself, but she could not persuade others to hire her to do it for them. Mary had learned how to convert old buildings into modern, attractive apartments that people would either rent or buy as condominiums. Mary had "fallen" into the business when she inherited an old, beat-up apartment building. Unable to sell it "as is," she blundered through a difficult, frustrating rehabilitation project. She finally sold the renewed building as condos, made a small profit, and in the process gained a valuable education.

She bought another old apartment building and struggled through the rehab process again. This time she sold her building for a larger profit. She continued, each time learning more about the complex rehab business—building regulations, financing, taxes, subcontracting, engineering and architecture, dealing with local government bureaucrats—all the elements that go into such projects.

Her tedious and exasperating experiences with each project taught her how to keep costs down, avoid problems, force fast action, and deal with local governments and banks. She learned how to manage, coordinate, and motivate egotistical architects, temperamental electricians, balky carpenters, skimping plumbers, and the like. She survived many bitter and disappointing experiences. After successfully rehabilitating ten properties, she considered herself an expert. Others agreed.

Several real estate brokers, knowing of Mary's work, asked her if she would consider rehabbing properties for prospective investors. Standing between these brokers and many lucrative sales of old, worn-out properties was the rehab process itself. Investors were not comfortable with the state of these buildings and would not buy without figuring out, in advance, how to get the rehabbing done without costly delays and budget overruns. These brokers viewed Mary's talent as their link to many profitable deals. All they had to do was convince investors that Mary could do the job. Mary was willing.

As a start, she and a broker associate teamed up to make a comprehensive presentation to an investor the broker had attracted to the idea of rehabbing the old West Hill Apartments. Mary's presentation detailed the process for the investor, including a summary of major pitfalls she had encountered in her own extensive experience. The presentation lasted more than an hour. At the end, the investor said that because he had some others in the deal with him, he needed a written proposal. She prepared and delivered a ten-page, single-spaced document that covered all the details of her oral presentation. It was nicely bound in an attractive cover and looked as professional as any document you would expect to see. Mary and the broker believed they were on target. In fact they were sure that the deal was "in the bag."

Instead, the proposal bombed, and the deal fell through. The investor said that he was just not convinced that the project was viable. He would not elaborate. The broker was perplexed. He could not understand why the investor had cooled on the deal. Nonetheless, the broker plowed ahead; he promptly found another prospect for the property. They went through the presentation again and followed up with the same written proposal. They bombed again. This time the prospective investor was somewhat more enlightening. He had not realized how complex, difficult, and risky the rehab process was until he had heard the presentation and read Mary's ten-page follow-up proposal. "Too complicated and too many pitfalls in the rehab process," he explained. Among other things, he could now see how the delaying tactics of some zoning officials, building inspectors, or architects who had no appreciation of the time-value of money could drain the profit out of an otherwise good deal.

Still undaunted, the broker continued his efforts, knowing that Mary's talents were outstanding and that with them many profitable deals could be put together. Again, he found another prospect for the West Hill property. "Persistence pays!" he said, enthusiastically. Mary, however, was concerned about the reasons for their two failures. She asked the broker to hold the prospect in abeyance, if he could, until she could collect herself.

By then Mary had reluctantly concluded that she was doing something wrong. After all, this deal was as good as the best of the many she had done for herself. She knew that people could make an attractive return on investment with very little risk. One fact remained. She had simply failed to do a good selling job. She and the broker had a good proposition in the West Hill project. Yet they had failed to persuade two different people who were looking for exactly what she could deliver. Therefore, the fault had to be hers.

Getting It All Together

To get help she decided to sign up for one of our seminar-workshops. She did her advance preparation by talking with the prospect, Greg Jefferson, the next person the broker had lined up for the West Hill project.

Using the Preparation Guidelines given in Chapter 1 to work up her own Outline Guide (Figure 11-1), Mary defined her objective clearly and wrote it in less than fifty words. This was Mary's message to Mary. It stated exactly what she wanted to accomplish with this persuasion task, and it was for her eyes only and not to be part of her proposal.

Her next task was to develop the needs of Greg Jefferson, the new prospect for the old West Hill property her broker had found. She and the broker met with Jefferson. But this time their approach was different. They said nothing about Mary's ability to coordinate a rehab project. Instead Mary spent the time developing Jefferson's needs. She also asked if there were others interested in the proposition. Jefferson said he usually involved his wife, his CPA, and sometimes his lawyer. With that she and the broker left, saying that they would submit a written proposal and follow up with another personal call. Jefferson agreed.

Using the process she had learned, Mary prepared her first proposal (see Figure 11-2). It worked. Mary got her first job as the coordinator of a rehab job for someone else. Her friend the real estate broker was in ecstasy as he calculated his commission. The technique she had learned and the single-page proposal she wrote served as the model for all the others she has since written in her prospering rehab business.

Mary and her associate, the real estate broker, completed the deal in a brief second meeting with Greg Jefferson. Jefferson commented that he had seen many proposals in his time, but this was one of the few that effectively covered a complex subject in one page. He expected that Mary's work on the West Hill project would be as effective. The real estate broker marveled at how Mary had boiled down her ten-page proposal into the essence that appeared in the final one-page letter.

Analyzing the Proposal

Now that you have read Mary's proposal, try analyzing it in terms of what you have learned. First, identify and mark the

(text continues on page 104)

Figure 11-1. The Anatomy of Persuasion Outline Guide.

AUDIENCE: Name the person(s) who can act on your proposal. { WIFE / LAWYER / CPA
  MR XXX — OWNER OF WEST HILL APARTMENTS

YOUR OBJECTIVE: State exactly what you want to accomplish as a result of this proposal (50 words or less).
  GET JOB OF COORDINATING THE WEST HILL PROJECT FROM BEGINNING TO END (OCCUPANCY)

NEED(s): Outline your audience's NEEDS as you believe he/she understands them. (Do you have agreement on these needs?)

1) *BUILD & RENT 42 UNITS—SHORTEST TIME—EFFICIENTLY*

2) *REDUCE RISK OF COSTLY MISTAKES*

3) *MAXIMIZE PROFITS*

PLAN: State what you propose your audience do to satisfy his/her needs (25 words or less).
  HIRE ME!

HOW-IT-WORKS: Outline how your PLAN will be carried out.

  FINANCIAL { *PRICING — CASHFLOW*
               TAXES — MORTGAGE
               COST — PROFITABILITY

  PLANS & CONST. { *MARKET — RENTS — ZONING*
                     LIAISON — ARCHITECTS/BUILDERS

  MARKETING { *STRATEGY — SAMPLE APARTMENT*
                ADVERTISING — TENANT SCREEN
                STAFFING

RESULTS: Outline what your audience will get in terms of benefits to satisfy his/her needs. (Couple the benefits with the NEEDS listed above.)

1) *MY EFFORT SAVES TIME — HANDLE TOTAL PROJECT*

2) *AVOID COSTLY MISTAKES*

3) *MAXIMIZE RETURN — GET JOB DONE ON TIME*

NEXT STEP: Request the action you want your audience to take. (Remember: a specific action by a specific time.)
  MEET MAY 4th TO FINALIZE / 10 AM?
  RÉSUMÉ? ADD TO HIW OR ATTACH

Please check your work against the structure and alignment chart.

Figure 11-2. Mary's proposal to coordinate a rehab job.

**WestView Properties
Mary Davis, President
1142 Maryland Avenue
Green Hills, NC 10024**

Mr. Gregory Jefferson
1001 Park Plaza
Greenville, Delaware 19896

Dear Mr. Jefferson:

As a follow-up to our meeting, our understanding is that your objective in the West Hill project is to create 42 rental units in the shortest possible time and most efficient manner, to avoid costly mistakes, and to realize the greatest profit.

I propose that you hire me to coordinate your project and to meet these objectives. The specific services I offer are these:

Financial: I will work with your accountant and attorney to develop cash-flow projections, tax-credit and shelter implications; help in obtaining mortgage financing and in analyzing mortgage options; examine construction cost projections in relation to the final value of the project, and make recommendations for cost-effectiveness.

Planning and Construction: I will do a neighborhood analysis for need and rent levels. Then I will meet with your architects to review how their designs meet these needs. I will coordinate planning, zoning, and historical designation requirements and also oversee the orderly flow of construction.

Marketing: I will develop a marketing strategy, including a sample unit, brochure, and other tools for obtaining qualified, quality tenants. I will also supervise the staffing and administration of the rent-up.

My qualifications: Have worked with city investors and rehabbers for ten years; own and operate 23 rental units for my own account; CCIM designation (Certified Commercial Investment Member); ongoing contacts with key personnel in city, county, and state government, also with attorneys, accountants, and bankers who specialize in real estate.

My efforts will save you time, reduce your risk of making costly mistakes, create a logical work flow, maximize your return, and get the job done on time.

I suggest that we finalize our agreement at a meeting on May 4th. I will call to confirm a time.

Cordially,

Mary Davis

---

various parts of the letter in terms of NEEDS, PLAN, HOW-IT-WORKS, RESULTS, and NEXT STEP. Turn back to the letter and test your skill before looking at Figure 11-3 to see how we have analyzed it.

Please note the paragraph citing her qualifications that Mary added to the HIW part. The question arises whether such information should be in HIW or form part of the attached materials. In this case, Mary stated her qualifications in less than fifty words so that there was no significant interruption in the thrust and flow of the proposal or any distraction in the decision-making process of the audience.

The Anatomy of Persuasion structure allows for flexibility. Information like Mary's qualifications can be inserted if care is taken not to divert the order of presentation away from the thrust and flow of the proposal. An attachment probably would have worked just as well and would have been a better solution if the information had been sufficiently long to have interrupted the flow of the prospect's thought processes.

Proposals can support a variety of attachments or other incidental information, ranging from something brief like Mary's short résumé to her ten-page, single-spaced proposal containing all the details of the West Hill rehab project and more. One of our participants regularly attaches 200-page documents to his single-page proposals. He does not interrupt the thrust and flow of the proposal because the persuasion process is completed one way or another in the proposal. If the proposal is successful, the persuaded audience will read, study, and digest any relevant attachment even if it is long and detailed. If unsuccessful, any attachment is usually irrelevant and useless. This is not to say that attachments are unimportant. They should be prepared with care. Poor work here can undo an otherwise successful effort.

Once you have mastered *The Anatomy of Persuasion* process, your skill will come from your ability to sort out and use what is important and essential to your audience and to discard what information is not. Mary did this very well once she had learned the process. She simply asked Greg Jefferson what his needs were. Then she decided what the essential elements were and included them. Once you have persuaded someone to buy into

Figure 11-3. Analysis of the parts of Mary's proposal letter.

WestView Properties
Mary Davis, President
1142 Maryland Avenue
Green Hills, NC 10024

Dear Mr. Jefferson:

NEEDS As a follow-up to our meeting, our understanding is that your objective in the West Hill project is to create 42 rental units in the shortest possible time and most efficient manner, to avoid costly mistakes, and to realize the greatest profit.

PLAN I propose that you hire me to coordinate your project and to meet these objectives. The specific services I offer are these:

HOW-IT-WORKS *Financial:* I will work with your accountant and attorney to develop cash-flow projections, tax-credit and shelter implications; help in obtaining mortgage financing and in analyzing mortgage options; examine construction cost projections in relation to the final value of the project and make recommendations for cost-effectiveness.

Planning and Construction: I will do a neighborhood analysis for need and rent levels. Then I will meet with your architects to review how their designs meet these needs. I will coordinate planning, zoning, and historical designation requirements and also oversee the orderly flow of construction.

Marketing: I will develop a marketing strategy, including a sample unit, brochure, and other tools for obtaining qualified, quality tenants. I will also supervise the staffing and administration of the rent-up.

My qualifications: Have worked with city investors and rehabbers for ten years; own and operate 23 rental units for my own account; CCIM designation (Certified Commercial Investment Member); ongoing contacts with key personnel in city, county, and state government, also with attorneys, accountants, and bankers who specialize in real estate.

RESULTS (Benefits) My efforts will save you time, reduce your risk of making costly mistakes, create a logical work flow, maximize your return, and get the job done on time.

NEXT STEP I suggest that we finalize our agreement at a meeting on May 4th. I will call to confirm a time.

Cordially,

Mary Davis

your proposition, that person will be willing to delve into the details.

Our next step is to go behind the scenes to examine Mary's preparation. She used the Outline Guide introduced at the beginning of this chapter. This is the form you can use to develop a proposal on any subject. It comes with directions you will readily understand now that you have come this far in your study of the persuasion process. The technique of outlining your thoughts in the briefest form will save you hours of useless writing.

As you examine Mary's work in Figure 11-1, you will see that she had picked up on Jefferson's comment about others in the AUDIENCE, namely, his wife, lawyer, and CPA.

She developed a clear OBJECTIVE, following the instructions to state what she wanted to accomplish *with this proposal* in fifty words or less. She wrote a clear statement that not only said what she wanted to do with this proposal but also defined the end point of the task she was proposing (occupancy). A mistake many beginners make is to write an objective that is too broad, one that extends beyond the immediate action wanted.

The NEED(s) part was done with very few words yet covered the subject competently. Because Mary and the broker had taken the time to meet with the prospective buyer of the West Hill Apartments, they had a clear understanding of Greg Jefferson's needs as he himself viewed them.

The PLAN, what Mary proposed that Jefferson do to satisfy his needs, in outline form was about as brief as possible: "Hire me!"

The HOW-IT-WORKS part was well outlined in three segments, with the barest of detail added to each. This worked well because Jefferson needed to know only that all bases would be covered competently. He did not want to be swamped by the horrendous detail involved in such projects. That was to be Mary's job. In fact, Mary's ten-page document had probably scared off her previous prospects.

Your skill in deciding what detail to include is critical. Too much is usually worse than too little. A general rule is to cover only the basic elements or issues involved. Then, if you have given too little information in an otherwise successful proposal, your audience is likely to identify the gap and ask you to fill it. This is much better than choking your audience and losing it right there. One more point on HIW: You can see from Mary's notes that she hesitated about what to do with her résumé. She decided to include in the proposal itself only a few words that would not interrupt the flow of her main thrust.

The RESULTS state what Jefferson will get in terms of *benefits* to satisfy his needs. Note that these are aligned (see the Second Alignment in Chapter 8) and connected with the needs. The NEXT STEP asks for specific action by a specific time, proposing a meeting on May 4 to finalize the deal.

Beginning Your Own Proposal

One objective of this book is to help you develop an actual proposal on a subject of your own choosing as you learn the principles of persuasion. A double benefit! You can produce something useful and learn a new skill simultaneously. You now have the basics of *The Anatomy of Persuasion*. You know the principles. As you go along, you will discover that this process is easy to understand, but it is not always easy to do. Therefore, the next three chapters will give you practice in building proposals based on information provided in each chapter. Meanwhile, as you do the practice assignment, start to develop your own proposal by using the Preparation Guidelines:

- Select a business or professional subject that is important to you personally.
- Pick a subject that is both important and timely, one that can be acted on soon.
- Define your objective in a clear, concise manner, and write it out in fifty words or less. This is your message to yourself. It should state exactly what you want to accomplish with this persuasion task. It is for your eyes only.
- Identify the needs of the person you wish to persuade. Be sure those needs reflect that person's views, not your own. (Your needs should be defined in your fifty-word objective statement.)

- Quantify important elements of your proposal, for example, costs, time, number of people required, quality, quantity or performance numbers, earnings, payback, and so forth.

You do not need to prepare a formal, finished proposal. The main thing is to be well informed on your subject. Keep it simple. Think carefully. Separate the important from the unimportant.

12

Case Study: How to Increase Staff During a Hiring Freeze

In this, the first of three practice assignments, you are to put yourself in Susan Albanese's place as a marketing executive. You are trying to persuade your boss, the marketing director, to let you employ someone at a time when the company is restricting new hires. You will use the Outline Guide. An answer sheet will give you extra guidance when you compare your work with Susan's.

The scenario: Susan manages the market research team in a small pharmaceutical company. During routine operations, Susan's group is composed of six people, each of whom studies various aspects affecting sales of the company's products. Over the years, many field salespeople began their careers as members of the team because it is an ideal career path to sales and management assignments. Thus the group serves as a pool for field sales candidates.

One of the six members of the team is a contractor hired two years ago when the company was "restructuring" and restricting new hires. The contractor, Sam Peterson, has become a valued contributor to the team's efforts despite one limitation: Company policy prevents him from having access to certain "need to know" proprietary information, which thus limits his assignments to less sensitive programs.

Ordinarily, the team's composition is ideal for the conduct

of its work. The company, however, is on the verge of getting FDA approval for a new drug that has the potential to capture one-third of the world market for treatment of hepatitis mainly because of the drug's lower-than-usual side effects. In addition to handling current market research work, Susan's team has been given the task of studying the market to decide how best to achieve maximum penetration in the shortest possible time. The team must present recommendations within three months.

To meet the deadline, Susan has decided to assign five of the team members to this single project because it has such an important bearing on the company's future. However, the contractor seems more of an impediment at this point because much of the new drug's technology is still available only on a "need to know" basis. Susan cannot be certain, if Sam is reserved for other ongoing programs, that he will only have nonsensitive projects to work on and she cannot use him to fill in for absent members of the team while they are working on the new drug program.

Susan knows that for some time there has been an open requisition to hire a sales candidate, but that because of the restructuring effort the requisition has gone unfilled. Susan has decided to propose to the marketing director that the requisition be filled by hiring Sam, who, in due course, would be the permanent replacement when one of the other team members is transferred to a field sales assignment.

YOUR ASSIGNMENT: Using the Outline Guide (Figure 12-1), prepare an outline for the proposal.

SUSAN'S OBJECTIVE: In this case, the objective for the proposal is given: Hire Sam, the independent contractor, as an employee.

Before looking at Figure 12-2 to compare your work with Susan's, please double-check what you have filled in. Have you carefully developed the NEEDS of your audience, the marketing director? Does the PLAN tell your audience what you want him to do to satisfy his needs? Does your HOW-IT-WORKS explain how the PLAN will be carried out? Do the RESULTS (benefits) tie in with the NEEDS by telling the marketing director exactly how the benefits will satisfy his specified needs? Finally, did you ask for specific action by a specific time in your NEXT STEP?

Figure 12-1. *The Anatomy of Persuasion* Outline Guide.

AUDIENCE: Name the person(s) who can act on your proposal.

YOUR OBJECTIVE: State exactly what you want to accomplish as a result of this proposal (50 words or less). _____

_____

_____

NEED(s): Outline your audience's NEEDS as you believe he/she understands them. (Do you have agreement on these needs?)
1) _____

2) _____

3) _____

PLAN: State what you propose that your audience do to satisfy his/her needs (25 words or less).

_____

_____

HOW-IT-WORKS: Outline how your PLAN will be carried out.

_____

_____

_____

_____

_____

RESULTS: Outline what your audience will get in terms of benefits to satisfy his/her needs. (Couple the benefits with the NEEDS listed above.)
1) _____

2) _____

3) _____

NEXT STEP: Request the action you want your audience to take. (Remember: a specific action by a specific time.)

_____

Please check your work against the Structure and Alignment Chart.

Figure 12-2. Susan's proposal outline answer sheet.

AUDIENCE: Name the person(s) who can act on your proposal.

The marketing director

YOUR OBJECTIVE: State exactly what you want to accomplish as a result of this proposal (50 words or less).

Hire Sam, the contractor, as a new employee.

NEED(s): Outline your audience's NEEDS as you believe he/she understands them. (Do you have agreement on these needs?)

1) Complete a marketing program for new drug within three months.
2) Stay current with all other business needs.
3) Maintain pool for field sales candidates.

PLAN: State what you propose that your audience do to satisfy his/her needs (25 words or less).

Use existing requisition to hire Sam as a new employee.

HOW-IT-WORKS: Outline how your PLAN will be carried out.

As a new employee, Sam will be used for ongoing projects.
Sam will also fill in on new drug project as needed.
Sam will replace person eventually transferred to sales.

RESULTS: Outline what your audience will get in terms of benefits to satisfy his/her needs. (Couple the benefits with the NEEDS listed above.)

1) New drug marketing plan completed on time.
2) Uninterrupted flow of ongoing programs.
3) Adequate personnel for field sales transfer.
4) Minimum training required.

NEXT STEP: Request the action you want your audience to take. (Remember: a specific action by a specific time.)

Extend job offer to Sam immediately.

The Alignment Exercise

With your proposal in outline form, you need to verify the logical relationships of each of the parts to ensure that your message will mesh with the decision-making process of the buying mind as did Susan's proposal. To do this, please recall the three alignments introduced in Chapter 8, Figure 8-1, and represented by the following chart (see Figure 12-3).

First Alignment

Susan's OBJECTIVE states what she wants to accomplish with this proposal. The PLAN, derived directly from her objective, tells what she proposes that the audience do to satisfy his needs. And

Figure 12-3. Structure and alignment chart.

STRUCTURE	ALIGNMENTS		
	(1)	**(2)**	**(3)**
AUDIENCE			
OBJECTIVE (yours in 50 words or less)	**OBJECTIVE** ↓		
NEEDS (Needs Agreement) (Yes or No)	↓	**NEEDS** ↓↑	
PLAN	**PLAN**		**PLAN** ↓↑
HIW	↓	↓↑	**HIW**
RESULTS		**RESULTS** (Benefits)	
NEXT STEP	**NEXT STEP**		

To analyze your proposal, check each of the three alignments separately against the Rules of Construction. When each alignment meets its rule, chances are that the whole proposal will work well when assembled. © 1993 the NEXT STEP asks the audience to take the specific action requested in the plan. There must be a logical flow of thought from OBJECTIVE through PLAN and on to NEXT STEP. This is absolutely critical. Proposals that do not have this logical flow are structurally weak and are likely to fail. Let's take a look at these three parts of Susan's proposal:

1. OBJECTIVE: Hire Sam, the contractor, as a new employee.
2. PLAN: Use existing requisition to hire Sam as a new employee.
3. NEXT STEP: Extend job offer to Sam immediately.

Happily, the flow is logical in this first alignment. The OBJECTIVE is to hire Sam. In the PLAN, Susan proposes that Sam be hired. The NEXT STEP asks that the job offer be made to Sam right away. It checks out; there are no nonsequiturs here, so we move on.

Second Alignment

This aligns and connects NEEDS and RESULTS (benefits). Remember, we are talking about the needs of the audience. Once you have established these, you are on firm ground. Then, after you present the PLAN to satisfy the prospect's NEEDS and explain how it works (HIW), you must connect the outcome, or RESULTS, with the NEEDS. This step is vitally important because it presents the benefits the audience will get and shows how these satisfy each need that was cited in the proposal. This connection must be firm and positive.

Let's examine the relationship between these two parts of Susan's proposal as we ask ourselves if each NEED of the audience seems to be satisfied by the RESULTS (benefits). For example, compare the first NEED ("Complete a marketing program for new drug within three months") with the first RESULT ("New drug marketing plan completed on time"). It jibes. The need is for a marketing plan for the new drug, and Susan's first result promised to fill the need by delivering such a plan on time. It works so far. Now, compare the rest of the needs and results. Is there a match?

Third Alignment

This aligns PLAN and HOW-IT-WORKS (HIW). HIW tells the audience, in principle, how the PLAN will be carried out, the plan being what the seller proposes that the buyer do to satisfy his or her needs, and HOW-IT-WORKS being an explanation of the plan in sufficient detail to provide the prospect with an understanding in principle of how the plan will be carried out. HIW does not call for a detailed elaboration, just a description in principle. Too much detail here can disrupt the flow of your proposal onto its most important part, RESULTS (benefits). Let's examine the match:

1. PLAN: Use existing requisition to hire contractor as a new employee.
2. HOW-IT-WORKS:
    (a) As a new employee, Sam will be used for ongoing projects.
    (b) Sam will also fill in on new drug project as needed.
    (c) Sam will replace person eventually transferred to sales.
    (d) After transfer of person to sales, we will engage new contractor.

As you examine HIW, ask yourself if what is given in the proposal contains enough information to explain what hiring Sam will mean to the workings of the group. What else, if anything, would you want to know if you were being asked to approve the hiring of Sam? If you can think of anything, now is the time to add it. How about some budget considerations? Would you need to know how much this new employee will be paid? Or, for budget reasons, would you want to know the effective date of his employment? This is a critical part of any proposal. You want to give just enough information to provide a basis for decision. If you overload here, you can confuse, distract, and divert your audience. The negative results of that are obvious.

How did you do? Before you answer that, please remember that your words need not exactly match the words Susan used. What counts is the thinking, the ideas you generate.

13

Case Study: How to Get Funding for Your Program

This, the second of three practice assignments, asks you to walk in Walt Bradley's shoes. Walt is the production manager in a plant producing a very profitable family of pressed wood products used primarily in new home construction. The plant has three production lines, each of which was added over a period of years as demand for the products increased. The forecast predicts further increases in demand, enough to exceed plant capacity in about one year. In anticipation, the company has developed new technology. With it, additional capacity will be gained at lower cost by upgrading the oldest of the existing three lines rather than building a fourth line.

Six months ago, management authorized $250,000 for planning the upgrade project. Walt's group used half these funds to develop the design and to estimate the final cost of the upgrade at $3 million. Just as this preliminary work was completed, a rise in interest rates caused an unexpected economic slump that hit the new housing market; sales dropped off significantly.

Although everyone expects the market to bounce back, Pete Sellers, company president, in a move to preserve cash, has ordered an immediate stop to all spending. He has ordered one of the three production lines to be shut down. He expects Walt to stop all activities involved in the upgrade project because the company will not need that capacity until about a year later than forecast.

While Walt needs to respond to Pete Sellers's directives, he realizes that a sudden, panic shutdown of the project team's efforts would be costly. Failing to complete certain critical designs would mean that much work would have to be repeated when the project was reactivated. This would waste both time and dollars. Consequently, when the housing market does revive, failure to meet the initial rush of orders would be costly in lost sales and earnings. If Walt can persuade Pete Sellers to let him complete another $50,000 of this critical work before shutting down, Walt could reactivate the upgrade project much faster when the time comes. This would allow Walt to get the new line operating at least two months earlier than if all efforts were dropped immediately. Two months' sales are worth $500,000 in earnings.

This proposed, short-term extension of the project would be used to complete all major equipment drawings and specifications, complete structural drawings, and order about $20,000 in long-term delivery items that will be critical to a rapid restart of the project.

YOUR ASSIGNMENT: Prepare an outline of a proposal to Pete Sellers.

OBJECTIVE: Get approval to finish critical parts of the upgrade project before shutting it down.

You will be using the Outline Guide (Figure 13-1) again. As before, when you finish, compare your work with Walt's.

Before looking at Figure 13-2, please double-check what you have put down. Have you carefully developed the NEEDS of your audience, Pete Sellers, company president? How about the PLAN? Does it tell Pete what you want him to do to satisfy his needs? Does your HOW-IT-WORKS tell how the plan will be carried out? Do the RESULTS (benefits) tie in with the NEEDS by explaining exactly how the benefits will satisfy those needs? Finally, did you ask for approval to go ahead?

The Alignment Exercise

With your proposal in outline form, you need to verify the logical relationships of each of the parts to ensure that your message will mesh with the decision-making process of the buying mind as

(text continues on page 120)

Figure 13-1. *The Anatomy of Persuasion* Outline Guide.

AUDIENCE: Name the person(s) who can act on your proposal.

YOUR OBJECTIVE: State exactly what you want to accomplish as a result of this proposal (50 words or less). _____

NEED(s): Outline your audience's NEEDS as you believe he/she understands them. (Do you have agreement on these needs?)
1) _____

2) _____

3) _____

PLAN: State what you propose that your audience do to satisfy his/her needs (25 words or less).

HOW-IT-WORKS: Outline how your PLAN will be carried out.

RESULTS: Outline what your audience will get in terms of benefits to satisfy his/her needs. (Couple the benefits with the NEEDS listed above.)
1) _____

2) _____

3) _____

NEXT STEP: Request the action you want your audience to take. (Remember: a specific action by a specific time.)

Please check your work against the structure and alignment chart.

Figure 13-2. Walt's proposal outline answer sheet.

AUDIENCE: Name the person(s) who can act on your proposal.

Pete Sellers, company president

YOUR OBJECTIVE: State exactly what you want to accomplish as a result of this proposal (50 words or less).

Get approval to finish critical parts of the upgrade project before shutting it down.

NEED(s): Outline your audience's NEEDS as you believe he/she understands them. (Do you have agreement on these needs?)

1) Preserve cash.
2) Be prepared to supply reviving market.
3) Maximize earnings.

PLAN: State what you propose that your audience do to satisfy his/her needs (25 words or less).

Approve completion of critical project tasks prior to shutdown.

HOW-IT-WORKS: Outline how your PLAN will be carried out.

Complete major equipment drawings and specifications.
Complete structural drawings.
Order long-term delivery items.
Suspend project work after additional $50,000 expenditure.

RESULTS: Outline what your audience will get in terms of benefits to satisfy his/her needs. (Couple the benefits with the NEEDS listed above.)

1) Saving of $75,000
2) Adequate capacity when market revives
3) Additional $500,000 in earnings
4) Avoidance of added expenses inherent in restarting project design

NEXT STEP: Request the action you want your audience to take. (Remember: a specific action by a specific time.)

Approve approximately $50,000 in added project work so design can continue without interruption.

did Walt's proposal. Again, look at the alignment chart. (Figure 13-3).

First Alignment

The OBJECTIVE states what Walt wants to accomplish with this proposal. The PLAN, derived directly from the objective, tells what Walt proposes that the audience do to satisfy his needs. The NEXT STEP asks the audience to take the specific action requested in the plan. There must be a logical flow of thought from OBJECTIVE through PLAN and on to NEXT STEP. This is absolutely critical.

Figure 13-3. Alignment chart.

STRUCTURE	ALIGNMENTS		
	(1)	**(2)**	**(3)**
AUDIENCE			
OBJECTIVE (yours in 50 words or less)	**OBJECTIVE** ↓		
NEEDS	↓	**NEEDS**	
(Needs Agreement) (Yes or No)		↓ ↑	
PLAN	**PLAN**		**PLAN** ↓ ↑
HIW	↓	↓ ↑	**HIW**
RESULTS		**RESULTS** (Benefits)	
NEXT STEP	**NEXT STEP**		

To analyze your proposal, check each of the three alignments separately against the Rules of Construction. When each alignment meets its rule, chances are that the whole proposal will work well when assembled.   © 1993

Second Alignment

This aligns and connects NEEDS and RESULTS (benefits). Remember, we are talking about the needs of the audience. Once you have established these, you have a firm foundation. Connecting the RESULTS with the NEEDS is vitally important because it presents the benefits that the audience will get and shows how these fill each need included in the proposal. The audience will visualize, feel, and understand exactly what the benefits are and exactly how these fill all the needs discussed.

Third Alignment

This aligns PLAN and HOW-IT-WORKS (HIW). The HIW part tells the audience, in principle, how the plan will be carried out. It does not call for a detailed elaboration—just a description in principle. Getting involved in detail here can divert your audience and disrupt the flow of your proposal onto its most important part—the RESULTS (benefits).

Epilogue

It seems that Pete Sellers's boss, Herman Walls, CEO of the company, has a habit of asking "offhand" questions. Sellers got where he is by providing succinct and correct answers. Sure enough, Walls asked if the upgrade project had been shut down. Your proposal, "replayed" in part by Pete, handled the question.

"Yes," Pete answered, "the project is shut down now except for one small part that will be finished shortly."

"What's that?"

"Walt is completing some design work. Doing it now instead of when we revive the project will save money by eliminating rework. This will speed the startup process, which could mean as much as $500,000 of increased earnings."

"Good," said Walls as he turned to another subject.

> **MORAL: Important parts of your audience may not always be in plain view.**

14

Case Study: How to Be a Rocket Scientist!

Let's try one more proposal. In this you become a rocket scientist whose name is Chris. Chris's task is to convince his boss to change the direction of the research at a critical juncture in an important project. The Outline Guide will escort you through this exercise again (Figure 14-1). An answer sheet will give you extra guidance as you compare your results with those of Chris. Chris has been assigned to conduct research on new plastics for use in nose cones on space vehicles. Recovery requires that vehicles survive the intense heat and pressure of reentry into the earth's atmosphere.

During his career in the plastics industry, Harry Jacobs, Chris's laboratory manager, has become widely respected for his many papers, patents, and industry awards. Harry is convinced that plastics are the answer and that a competent scientist like Chris is sure to solve the problem. Material specs must be firmed up in the next nine months because, at that time, all candidate materials must be ready for flight test in space on a scheduled shuttle flight. Only six materials can be included in the test.

Now, at the end of four months, Chris has screened hundreds of plastics, but found only six that barely survived laboratory tests. His judgment tells him that the candidates will not meet performance criteria in space and that he will be no closer to solving the problem if he continues to test plastic materials.

Meanwhile, Chris has learned of new composite materials that combine plastics and ceramics. These are foamed into light-

Figure 14-1. *The Anatomy of Persuasion* Outline Guide.

AUDIENCE: Name the person(s) who can act on your proposal.

YOUR OBJECTIVE: State exactly what you want to accomplish as a result of this proposal (50 words or less). ⎯⎯⎯⎯⎯⎯⎯

NEED(s): Outline your audience's NEEDS as you believe he/she understands them. (Do you have agreement on these needs?)

1) ⎯⎯⎯⎯⎯⎯⎯

2) ⎯⎯⎯⎯⎯⎯⎯

3) ⎯⎯⎯⎯⎯⎯⎯

PLAN: State what you propose that your audience do to satisfy his/her needs (25 words or less).

HOW-IT-WORKS: Outline how your PLAN will be carried out.

RESULTS: Outline what your audience will get in terms of benefits to satisfy his/her needs. (Couple the benefits with the NEEDS listed above.)

1) ⎯⎯⎯⎯⎯⎯⎯

2) ⎯⎯⎯⎯⎯⎯⎯

3) ⎯⎯⎯⎯⎯⎯⎯

NEXT STEP: Request the action you want your audience to take. (Remember: a specific action by a specific time.)

Please check your work against the Structure and Alignment Chart.

weight, strong structures that have extreme temperature and pressure resistance capabilities, at least under some laboratory test conditions. Chris is excited about the prospects for success with composites and sure that he can find at least six candidates in time for the shuttle flight test. To meet the schedule, Chris needs all the time remaining to concentrate on screening composites.

Chris has reviewed the results of his work on plastics to date with Harry. He believes that you are too pessimistic and that at least three of the plastic candidates may do well under flight test conditions. With five months still to go before flight test, he believes Chris is likely to find still better plastic candidates.

YOUR ASSIGNMENT: Prepare an outline for Chris's persuasion task.

OBJECTIVE: To increase the probability of solving the space vehicle materials problem.

Before looking at Figure 14-2 to compare your work with Chris's, please double-check. Have you carefully developed Harry's NEEDS? How about the PLAN? Does it tell Harry what you want him to do to satisfy his needs? Does your HOW-IT-WORKS describe how the plan will be carried out? Do the RESULTS (benefits) tie in with the NEEDS by telling exactly how the benefits will satisfy Harry's needs? Finally, did you ask for approval to go ahead?

The Alignment Exercise

Again, because it is vitally important to your success, you need to verify the logical relationship of each of the parts of your proposal outline to ensure that your message will mesh with the decision-making process of the buying mind as did Chris's proposal. Please revisit the chart (Figure 14-3).

First Alignment

The OBJECTIVE states what Chris wants to accomplish with this proposal. The PLAN, derived directly from your objective, tells

Figure 14-2. Chris's proposal outline answer sheet.

AUDIENCE: Name the person(s) who can act on your proposal.

Harry Jacobs

YOUR OBJECTIVE: State exactly what you want to accomplish as a result of this proposal (50 words or less).

To increase the probability of solving the space vehicle materials problem.

NEED(s): Outline your audience's NEEDS as you believe he/she understands them. (Do you have agreement on these needs?)

1) To meet project objectives, performance, and schedule.
2) To be comfortable with the solution.
3) To use sound research protocol.

PLAN: State what you propose that your audience do to satisfy his/her needs (25 words or less).

Agree to screen composites during the remainder of laboratory program.

HOW-IT-WORKS: Outline how your PLAN will be carried out.

1) Already have isolated best of plastics.
2) Screen and isolate best of preferred composites.
3) Select best six from among both plastics and composites for flight-test on schedule.

RESULTS: Outline what your audience will get in terms of benefits to satisfy his/her needs. (Couple the benefits with the NEEDS listed above.)

1) Have six materials ready for flight-test on schedule.
2) Plastics will be integral part of solution.
3) Will have evaluated broadest possible technical solutions.

NEXT STEP: Request the action you want your audience to take. (Remember: a specific action by a specific time.)

Approve immediate change in program to include tests for composites.

Figure 14-3. Alignment chart.

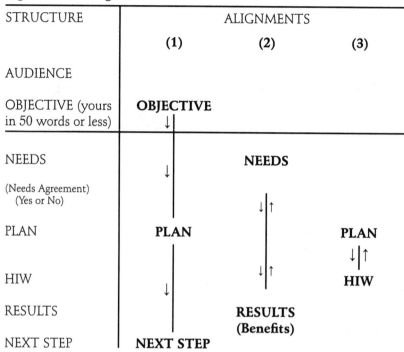

STRUCTURE	ALIGNMENTS		
	(1)	**(2)**	**(3)**
AUDIENCE			
OBJECTIVE (yours in 50 words or less)	**OBJECTIVE** ↓		
NEEDS	↓	**NEEDS**	
(Needs Agreement) (Yes or No)		↓ ↑	
PLAN	**PLAN**		**PLAN** ↓ ↑
HIW	↓	↓ ↑	**HIW**
RESULTS		**RESULTS** (Benefits)	
NEXT STEP	**NEXT STEP**		

To analyze your proposal, check each of the three alignments separately against the Rules of Construction. When each alignment meets its rule, chances are that the whole proposal will work well when assembled.   © 1993

what Chris proposes that the audience do to satisfy his needs. The NEXT STEP asks the audience to take the specific action requested in the plan. There must be a logical flow of thought from OBJECTIVE through PLAN and onto NEXT STEP. This is absolutely critical.

Second Alignment

This aligns and connects NEEDS and RESULTS (benefits). Remember, we are talking about the needs of the audience. Once you have established these, you are on firm ground. Connecting the RESULTS with the NEEDS is vitally important because it presents the benefits that the audience will get and shows how these fill each need included in the proposal. The audience will visualize, feel, and understand exactly what the benefits are and exactly how these fill all the needs discussed.

Third Alignment

This aligns PLAN and HOW IT WORKS (HIW). The HIW part tells the audience, in principle, how the plan will be carried out. It does not call for a detailed elaboration—just a description in principle. Getting involved in detail here can divert your audience and disrupt the flow of your proposal onto its most important part—the RESULTS (benefits).

Epilogue

This exercise illustrates how you can sometimes overcome a mind-set by simply jumping over it. In this case, Harry Jacobs was set on using plastics. We can understand that because we all like to deal with matters about which we are well informed. Chris, on the other hand, could see that Harry's strong preference for plastics would give way if it jeopardized success. So Chris decided to get Harry to agree that the end was more important than the means. In short, he jumped over Harry's prejudice in favor of plastics by focusing his attention on the "big picture."

You will find many opportunities to use this technique because it gets back to the foundation—your analysis of a person's needs. Here there was a choice. Harry needed to be successful more than he needed to use plastics. Q.E.D.

15

Building Your Own Proposal

If you have come this far, the probability is that you have reconfirmed your need to improve your persuasion skills and wish to forge ahead. If so, let's take a moment to review where you are right now.

- You know the mental process we all use whenever we make a decision to buy or not to buy anything (NEED, RECOGNITION, SEARCH, EVALUATION, and DECISION).
- You know that to be successful your message must mesh with, complement, nurture, and influence that process.
- By using the Outline Guide, you know exactly how to structure your messages so as to make this happen (AUDIENCE OBJECTIVE, NEEDS, NEEDS AGREEMENT, PLAN, HOW-IT-WORKS, RESULTS [benefits], and NEXT STEP).
- You probably agree that you lack only experience in building proposals and the reinforcing satisfactions that come with success after success after success.

So, if you agree that this is an accurate assessment of your situation, I propose that you start correcting both shortfalls by building your own proposal.

How-It-Works

You begin by following the Preparation Guidelines mentioned in Chapter 1. Please choose a subject on which to develop your proposal.

Step 1

Select a business or professional subject for your persuasion task if possible. Here are some suggestions to start you off. You may have ideas on how to improve your company's business or its operation: a new personnel policy, a new marketing plan, a cost reduction program, a new product research project, a major capital investment in high-tech equipment, a novel customer relations policy, a pricing change, an effort to improve quality, a new financial management method.

Or perhaps you want approval to change a manufacturing process or to reorganize the field sales force so as to reduce the high cost of selling. Perhaps you wish to propose to your board of directors a merger of your company with another. Or maybe you want to broaden your authority, get a promotion, a raise, or a change of assignment.

Perhaps you want to recruit a person to work for your company. You may want to make a substantial change in a major, ongoing project that will add cost but will save money in the long run. Perhaps you have to justify or defend a decision. Maybe your task is to gain agreement for a change in the rules or regulations of an organization. You may need management approval for an increased advertising budget.

Or you may need the consensus of your peers, people with whom you work such as a committee or a board of directors. Whatever subject you select, be sure it is a *real* and not a hypothetical situation.

Step 2

Pick a persuasion task that is both important and timely, one that can be acted on soon. You will get more skill development from your efforts and produce a more effective result if your selection is the most important task you will be facing in the near future. You will apply more care and diligence to the proposal if, besides being especially important to you, it also has urgency or at least a deadline attached to it. The benefit here is that you will see and feel your success early on, because you will go full cycle in a relatively short time.

Step 3

Define your audience. Name the person or persons to whom you
will address this proposal. Do you know all you need to know
or at least all you can know about this person? Be sure that this
person has the authority to act on your proposal. Keep in mind
any other people who might be influential. Recall that Mary
Davis, in Chapter 11, realized that her prospect, Greg Jefferson,
also had a wife, a lawyer, and a CPA "peering" over his
shoulder.

Step 4

*Define your objective in a clear, concise manner and write it in fifty
words or less.* State exactly what *you* want to accomplish as a
result of *this* proposal. Allow me to reemphasize here that this
statement of objective is to govern this proposal only. It focuses
on the immediate task; it defines the action you wish to get with
this proposal and nothing more.

Remember that your objective statement is *your* message to
you. It is the essential control element of your effort. It is for your
eyes only. It will not be included in your version of your proposal as presented to your audience. The fifty-word constraint
is important. With all due respect, if you cannot define your
objective clearly and completely in fifty words, you probably
have not thought it through.

After you have developed your objective, test it by *thinking
beyond the thing itself.* Remember Jim Weston from Chapter 8.
You will recall that when Weston presented his proposal to the
seminar-workshop group, he said that his objective was to persuade his boss to approve the construction of an elevator *(the
thing)* so as to move both people and product in a faster, cheaper,
and safer way. Another participant, thinking beyond the thing
itself, suggested that the result was Jim's real objective, not the
elevator per se.

At first Jim disagreed, insisting that the elevator was what
he wanted. Finally, when someone asked him if he would still
want the elevator if he could accomplish the same task by another means, Jim was able to think *beyond the thing itself* and to

view his objective differently, allowing the elevator to become the means instead of the end. The result was that Jim Weston gained better control of his thought processes as he developed his proposal. He might have gone even further. Suppose that moving people and product safer, faster, and cheaper would result in breaking a costly bottleneck, one that would reduce production costs. Then Jim Weston might have written his objective as follows:

> To get approval for a plan to reduce production costs by 0.5 percent and increase safety by moving people and product between the first and second floors with a new elevator (31 words).

Thinking beyond the thing itself is good practice and should be done routinely. As you write your objective, ask yourself: If my proposal is accepted, what will the outcome be for me? Is this all I want out of my proposal? Am I defining the *end* I want or just the means? Jim did not really want an elevator for its own sake; he did not even want to move people and product faster. Rather, when boiled down, he defined his real objective to reduce costs and increase safety. As a routine exercise, before you set your objective, survey your situation by running your ideas through this process. If your observations do not produce improving results, stay where you are.

Step 5

Identify the needs of the person(s) you wish to persuade. This aspect of the persuasion process deserves your undivided attention and analysis. There is, however, one caveat: Be sure the needs you write down reflect the views of that person and not your own. Your needs are defined in your fifty-word objective statement.

You may think that this caveat is absolutely unnecessary. In fact you may consider it insulting. If so, please forgive me, and let me tell you that most of us, on occasion, fail to completely separate our needs from those of the person to be persuaded. True empathy is difficult to achieve. This is a common human failing. But, at this point, your needs are not important. You are trying to fill the needs of your audience. Remember, you are trying to persuade; you are not trying to negotiate. These are two different processes. Finally, you can never know too much about the needs of the person you are trying to persuade.

Step 6

Quantify important elements of your proposal, for instance, costs, time, number of people required, quality, quantity or performance numbers, earnings, payback, and so forth. Think it through. Do the research. If there is any place for overkill, it is on research of this kind. This is not to say that you will cram huge quantities of information into your proposal. To the contrary. By having a wealth of data, you will be able to select and use only the most essential items in your proposal. You will also be fully prepared to handle questions and any elaboration of details that may be called for later.

Another caveat: Handle quantified information with great care. Decide how your audience will react to the information you have developed. What seems big to me may seem trivial to you and vice versa. For example, you may recall the battle for long-distance telephone business between AT&T and MCI done with TV commercials. AT&T apparently wanted to stem the tide of people switching to MCI. To do this, AT&T ran a commercial that showed the hands of a magician manipulating a one-dollar bill. He rolled the bill into a tube and concealed it in his closed hand. Then he opened his hand to reveal that the dollar bill had turned into three pennies. I believe the intended message was that switching to MCI was hardly worth the trouble. After all, who would want to switch long-distance carriers for a mere three cents?

On the other hand, the message may have boomeranged. What are three pennies? Trivia? Yes, maybe. But the AT&T commercial related the three pennies to a dollar bill. That is 3 percent. And that can be quite a lot, depending on how one thinks about it. Suppose your company spends $10,000 a month on long distance phone and fax messages; 3 percent is $3,600 per year. Or maybe your company spends a million dollars a year; 3 percent is $30,000. Suppose someone suggests that from now on you increase your tipping in restaurants from 15 to 18 percent. Quickly, what does that amount to in a year? If you do a lot of entertaining in business, consider the tax implications of an additional 3 percent. Would you give a real estate broker 9 percent instead of the customary 6 percent to sell your home?

Some Final Cautions

As you work on your preparation, remember that you do not have to write anything except informal notes. In short, just be extremely well informed on the subject you have chosen. Once you have completed your preparation, you are ready to apply your information to the Outline Guide. *Keep it brief.* There is not much room for detail on the Outline Guide. Mary Davis's Outline Guide (Chapter 11) is a good example.

As an aside, can you remember the times you have tried to pull together a proposal or a presentation and found yourself wallowing in pages and pages of materials you had created? You stared at the work wondering how you could bring order out of this self-inflicted chaos and pull it all together into a cogent message. If this dilemma is familiar, you are typical of most people. Nearly everyone can recall unpleasant memories of this sort. But you can avoid it completely with the approach you are taking. By just making notes, the briefest of notes, and not allowing yourself to write a tome, you will keep your thinking concise. The Outline Guide will keep your thinking organized. So, with concise, well-organized information, you will stay on target with remarkable efficiency of thought. Therefore, you will not be faced with the task of boiling down a lot of confusing written material—because you will not create it in the first place.

Remember, there is no substitute for careful, diligent preparation. Ask any lawyer who has tried to persuade a jury about the importance of thorough preparation.

With the Outline Guide completed, all you will need to do is flesh out your work to suit whatever mode of delivery you have chosen—a group presentation, a face-to-face situation, a concise, single-page memo, a letter, an advertisement, or any other format, even audiovisual media.

The Results

A double reward awaits you. With a single effort, you will have learned the basics of a lifetime skill, and simultaneously you will have developed a real proposal to get the action you have in mind. Success! We can say congratulations in advance with confidence, because we know that all you have to do is follow the rules you have learned as you think your way through the development of your proposal. We know this because participants in *The Anatomy of Persuasion* seminars report back on their immediate successes. Other participants whom we bump into years later tell us that they have continued to use *The Anatomy of Persuasion* principles because they work. Your next step is to use the Outline Guide (Figure 15-1) and get started with your first proposal.

Epilogue

Your skill will increase with experience. Here is a way you can accelerate the process. After each persuasion task you undertake, win or lose, take a few minutes to analyze and make note of the outcome. You now know the mechanics of the process of persuasion. Therefore, you can easily figure out what worked, what didn't, and *why.*

As you continue building experience, you will notice that your accumulated knowledge will guide you. You will have a much better sense of the reality of any given situation. Your mind will penetrate beneath the surface. Your instincts will sharpen. And your batting average will increase for two reasons: (1) You will be able to exploit potential winning situations, and (2) you will be able to identify and avoid situations that are potential losers.

Persuasion is not easy. Like any other action that requires high skill, it just looks easy when you observe an expert in action. So if you find this work difficult, join the crowd. But take heart, the principles you learn here will make persuasion very much easier for you. Some time down the line, you will be mak-

Figure 15-1. *The Anatomy of Persuasion* Outline Guide.

AUDIENCE: Name the person(s) who can act on your proposal.

YOUR OBJECTIVE: State exactly what you want to accomplish as a result of this proposal (50 words or less). ———————————————

NEED(s): Outline your audience's NEEDS as you believe he/she understands them. (Do you have agreement on these needs?)

1) ————————————————————————————

2) ————————————————————————————

3) ————————————————————————————

PLAN: State what you propose that your audience do to satisfy his/her needs (25 words or less).

HOW-IT-WORKS: Outline how your PLAN will be carried out.

RESULTS: Outline what your audience will get in terms of benefits to satisfy his/her needs. (Couple the benefits with the NEEDS listed above.)

1) ————————————————————————————

2) ————————————————————————————

3) ————————————————————————————

NEXT STEP: Request the action you want your audience to take. (Remember: a specific action by a specific time.)

Please check your work against the Structure and Alignment Chart.

ing it look easy to others who will be amazed at your grasp of the persuasion process.*

Summary

Here's what you do in a nutshell:

- Select a business or professional subject for your persuasion task if possible.
- Pick a persuasion task that is both important and timely, one that can be acted on soon.
- Define your audience.
- Define your objective in a clear, concise manner, and write it in fifty words or less.
- Identify the needs of the person(s) you wish to persuade.
- Quantify important elements of your proposal, e.g., costs, time, number of people, quality, quantity or performance numbers, earnings, payback, and so on.
- Use the Outline Guide to develop your proposal.

---

*Pop Quiz: Take a look back at this chapter. Can you identify the structure: NEEDS, PLAN, HOW IT WORKS, RESULTS, and NEXT STEP?

16

A Touch of the Real World

Just as we absorb the basics of something new, just as we become skilled enough to enjoy our accomplishment and dare to venture forth, we are promptly disabused by practical experience. But, if we are well grounded in the basics, we soon rise from rookie to professional competence by learning to cope with reality. So it is with persuasion skills.

Although experience is a great teacher, forewarning can lessen the impact of the nasty surprises, disruptions, and irregularities so generously meted out by those we wish to persuade. This chapter offers samples of a few of the kinds of situations you may face. There are also some helpful advisories on situation variants that I like to call The Strange, The Unpredictable, The Preoccupied, The Impossible, and The Complicated.

The Strange

"Other" people prioritize needs in very strange ways. What is pure lunacy to you and to me may be rational and normal to others. For example, you and I do not understand why some people are more interested in whether the Jacksonville Sharks beat the Toronto Tarantulas than they are in whether Congress is really going to impeach the president this week or vice versa.

Don't try to convince the sales VP of a certain large company to hold the semiannual sales meeting at any place that doesn't have a championship golf course unless you are his boss. Even though most of the 150 people attending such meetings don't play golf, he claims consensus as he regularly imposes his day of golf on the group, no matter what.

> **Advisory: Try to acclimate yourself to the idiosyncrasies, peculiarities, and eccentricities of others. Remember, the "customer is always right," even when you know he or she is wrong.**

The Unpredictable

Some things are beyond the pale. Once we had a date to make a presentation to a highly placed prospect named Jack, who was director of human resources at a rapidly growing company. We really didn't know this person at all, so, hoping to get better acquainted, we decided to take Jack to lunch beforehand. Unfortunately, we picked a five-star hotel with a fine French restaurant. Jack ordered a double martini. He swilled it down and ordered another. He swilled that down too. Upon the arrival of his first course, vichyssoise, he asked for catsup to add to it. Word got to the kitchen fast. The chef, taking umbrage, served the catsup himself. With it he muttered a slur about wanting to meet the "person" who would put catsup in *"his"* vichyssoise. Jack, fueled by the martinis, went ballistic and stalked out of the restaurant. We were nonplussed. Our proposal was postponed, to say the least. If only we had chosen McDonald's. . . .

Eventually, we all must deal with the curious behavior of a certain breed of leader. These are the stalwarts who try to cure inherent defects with radical change. They orchestrate sweeping reorganizations, mergers, acquisitions, downsizings, upsizings, and the like. The resulting internal disturbances usually mask the real problems.

For the would-be persuaders, these situations create serious impediments, if not impassable roadblocks. For example, once we thought we were about to sign up a large accounting firm. The idea was to put all the managers and partners through our seminar-workshop so that they could, with improved powers of persuasion, mend their sagging relationships with clients and get sorely needed new business.

Because this firm had grown bloated with overhead, its fees had become excessive. Smaller CPA firms had slowly stripped clients away, one at a time, by doing the same work at lower cost. The damage, like cancer, went unnoticed in the early stages. The leaders of this big firm had cloistered themselves from reality. They had consistently ignored warnings from the lower eche- lons. Finally, however, they recognized that they needed to be- come competitive.

We believed that our proposal was all but signed and sealed, that the managing partners had already agreed that most of their people really did need to improve their persuasion skills, and that our seminar-workshop would be a giant step toward solving the problem. We were salivating, being sure a nice piece of business would be ours. But, the day before our final meeting, *The Wall Street Journal* alerted us to trouble. It was an article announcing the forthcoming merger of this and an- other large CPA firm. The leaders apparently thought that get- ting bigger (instead of smarter) was a better solution to their dilemma.

Bombing the main office of this accounting firm could not have done more damage. Everything stopped. Insecurity reigned. The work flow suffered as employees, knowing that their jobs were in jeopardy, worried about their futures. The stress level went through the roof. Our proposal bogged down deeply in this dismal atmosphere as the copy machines cranked out résumés by the hundreds. Meanwhile, we went on to other things.

For more than a year the people in the two almost-merged firms did not know what the next day would bring. Incidentally, the powers finally aborted the merger plan. The toll of this caper was incalculable. These leaders lost tons of business, good will for their firms, and the loyalty of their employees.

Of course, it doesn't take a merger to cause disqualifying trouble for you and your proposal. Even relatively minor per- sonnel changes can be devastating. The appointment of a new manager or group head may be disruptive enough to derail your proposal. Agendas change, needs change, and the periods of re- covery can sometimes be long.

Advisory: The more you know about the people you wish to persuade, the less likely you are to be tripped up by their fancies and foibles or surprised by their whims. And, don't count your chickens. . . .

The Preoccupied

Diversions change people's needs suddenly. Take the case of J. Upton Peerless, CEO and dominating figure in a major corporate refinancing project that will affect thousands of stockholders. You, working closely with Mr. Peerless, have *almost* sold him on your plan to carry out this large and important task. You are to provide Mr. Peerless with the one last piece of documentation he says he urgently needs to finalize and announce his go decision. You have prepared the data personally; you have the documentation in hand; you are ready; this is to be your day. You expect that your meeting with Mr. Peerless will be little more than a formality, like cutting a ribbon to open a new building or highway. He will receive the critical document from you. Then, with a flourish and splash of enthusiasm, he will set the project in motion, and you will be a winner with your implementation plan as the heartbeat of the project. Voilà!

At the crucial meeting, you present the document to Mr. Peerless. Instead of the expected enthusiasm and flourish, you get a ho-hum reaction. He is inexplicably vague. His eyes seem rheumy. It is as though you are talking to a zombie. He waves you off, telling you to check back next week. You are stunned, flabbergasted! What you don't know, and may never know, is the cause of Peerless's bizarre behavior. Perhaps his doctor zinged him with a message about some needed surgery. Maybe it was a surprise call from his wife's lawyer announcing divorce proceedings. Or maybe he is full of pain killer to control an attacking kidney stone. Who knows?

Advisory: Personal matters can intervene with devastating impact and quickly bend even the most exalted out of shape. You must decide whether to wait

patiently for another shot or pack up and go elsewhere. These can be tough calls sometimes.

The Impossible

When your boss (or your boss's boss) recognizes that you have exceptional skill in developing proposals, you may be recruited to help sell one of his/her ideas to higher management. If the idea has merit and is likely to be a winner if properly promoted, you may be in clover. But if the idea, product, or service your boss wishes to advance is a poor one and likely to lose, you may be facing a career-damaging situation. Just as standing near a mud puddle is risky, mere association with an unsound project is more than just undesirable. You can be sure a scapegoat will be designated and, ten to one, it will not be your boss.

Here's a scenario: Your boss asks you to help develop a proposal to higher management. The idea appears to you to be of dubious value at best and as downright unworkable at worst. Upon closer examination you decide the faults are so obvious that only morons would buy into it. Remember Ford's Edsel and the new Coke! But like it or not, when you participate, you are involved. Your name is on the thing, whatever it is.

> **Advisory: Ask leading questions about higher management's needs and how this idea will fill them. Try to get your boss to see the fallacies. Then turn your persuasion skill on your boss very gently. With luck, you may be able to convince your boss to junk the idea before higher management does it for him/her. Remember: The butt you save may be your own.**

The Complicated

We can divide The Complicated into two broad categories, cases 1 and 2. The first occurs when many complex, interrelated needs are involved in a given situation. Some of the needs may seem to be offsetting, compensating, or even opposing the others.

They are characteristically difficult to sort out. Your task is to get agreement on the needs. To do this you will learn to analyze, summarize, and thus bring order out of the complication.

The second is when you have no direct input about your audience's needs. You must assume the needs of your audience because you have no way to confirm them directly. Advertisers face this problem routinely. Obviously, advertisers cannot query every reader or viewer about his/her needs. They must assume that certain people in the audience will have certain needs. They develop the needs by using focus groups or by other sampling techniques. If you want to advertise to physicians, you would study the needs of physicians until you felt you knew enough about doctors to address them through advertising.

Case 1

Sometimes the needs are complicated so that you require astute analytical skill in presenting a proposal that deals with the complexities in a concise, easy-to-understand manner. This time you are selling heavy industrial equipment used in chemical manufacturing.

Let's review your conversations with Al Fresco, the director of purchasing for Golden-Gro, a company that makes lawn and garden fertilizers. This is a highly competitive, cost-sensitive, low-margin commodity business. Management keeps a tight reign on all costs. Mill costs, the cost of manufacturing, get extra special scrutiny. This is because of one critical piece of manufacturing equipment—a chemical reactor that breaks down frequently. This happens because the manufacturing people push it beyond its limits. They try to keep mill costs low by deliberately overloading the chemical reactor during periods of peak demand. They hope that the extra production gained will offset the cost of the inevitable breakdown.

Replacing the chemical reactor is not indicated for two reasons. The cost of a new, more reliable unit would be too high considering that repairs on the present equipment are relatively easy. The cost of new parts is low and the installation task is uncomplicated. The catch is that each repair job requires at least a twenty-four-hour shutdown. But management agrees that a better way to ensure economical production is needed. It wants to get a backup system to partially relieve the impact of the inevitable shutdowns. Al Fresco's bosses impose stringent requirements on his purchasing task.

Even though the capacity of the backup can be lower than that of the main reactor, the backup must be absolutely reliable and must turn out product of equal or better quality and at a lower cost than the main reactor does. Management is wary of new equipment trials because other suppliers have been allowed to conduct tests in this plant, and nothing useful has resulted so far. Worse, production time lost has been costly. Therefore, management will not allow other tests unless success is assured. Accordingly, nothing short of a complete assurance in advance that you can meet the requirements will be acceptable. Al's last words emphasize the point. "They will not spend valuable plant time on experiments."

You are not absolutely positive that your backup chemical reactor, called the Quantum System, will make the Golden-Gro product to quality and cost specifications. You have been successful with similar operations but not with anything identical to Golden-Gro's.

After pondering this somewhat complicated situation, you decide on a two-step approach to meet Golden-Gro's needs. As a first step, you will run a preliminary test in your laboratory to establish that you can actually make their product satisfactorily with the Quantum System. Then you will propose an actual production test of the Quantum System at the Golden-Gro plant. *Because this task is costly for you, you will ask Al Fresco to agree in advance to purchase your Quantum System at a price previously discussed, provided that you can duplicate your laboratory test in Golden-Gro's production environment.*

As you develop your proposal, you discover that the NEEDS part is fairly easy to write. Golden-Gro knows what it needs and so do you.

The PLAN part is a bit tricky because you are asking for a commitment to buy in advance of the demonstration but contingent on that demonstration being successful. Holding to the twenty-five-word constraint may be difficult here, but you will try. This statement must be absolutely clear even if you are forced to use a few extra words.

The HOW-IT-WORKS part really has two parts. First Golden-Gro must understand how the laboratory test will be carried out and how the results will be presented. You will produce actual product made from company ingredients in addition to a written report detailing temperatures, pressures, and energy consumption, plus your projections as to how the full-scale production run should turn out. Golden-Gro must also understand that success in your lab will meet the first of its needs and will commit the company to moving on to the production run in its own plant.

The RESULTS (benefit) part merely plays back Golden-Gro's needs in terms of what it will get.

You decide to call Al to tell him that you have prepared a written proposal for him to take to his management. You also ask Al if you can take five minutes of his time to read him the proposal over the phone to be sure it accurately reflects the situation as he sees it.

Figure 16-1 presents the single-page proposal you prepared that will lead to the sale of your Quantum System. Incidentally, Al Fresco liked the conciseness and brevity of your proposal because he usually gets long, complicated proposals from other suppliers on much less complex subjects, which Golden-Gro's management refuses to read. So he must take time to boil down such proposals himself. He is thinking of demanding single-page proposals from all his suppliers in the future. Furthermore, he used your letter to get approval from his management. He sold them in ten minutes. The tests also went well, and you made the sale.

Case 2

Now let's examine a situation in which you have no personal access to your audience. In such cases you are forced to assume the needs of your audience and to build your proposal accordingly. *Empathy* is the operative word here. To become empathic, you must put yourself in the other person's position. Marketers of new products often use focus groups to synthesize the actual

Figure 16-1. Proposal for selling heavy industrial equipment used in chemical manufacturing.

Quantum Systems, Inc.
321 Ponce de Leon Boulevard
Jacksonville, Florida XXXXX
Tel.: (XXX)-XXX-XXXX

Mr. Al Fresco
Golden-Gro Products Company
Sunnyside, Florida XXXXX

Dear Al:

This is to summarize the needs of Golden-Gro that we discussed yesterday. You said that the chemical reactor in your production sequence is unreliable and that you need a backup system to overcome this shortfall. You also said that management will not consider any backup system, even for trial, unless it offers a realistic promise of both reliability and cost reduction.

To satisfy these needs, I propose that Golden-Gro agree to buy our Quantum System if we complete a two-step program to prove its value in use. Here is how the program would be carried out:

Step 1 will be a *laboratory study*. Using samples of your actual ingredients, we will run a pilot production test at our laboratory. If successful, the finished product together with a written report will be prepared for you. Then, with your agreement, we will jointly present the results to your management to gain approval for Step 2.

Step 2 will be a *full-scale production run* at the Golden-Gro plant to confirm the Step 1 results. We will provide all equipment and technical assistance for Step 2.

Experience at other plants has shown the Quantum System to be inexpensive to install and easy to use. Typical savings in processes similar to yours are $98 per ton of ingredient and a 10 percent reduction in energy costs.

Results: The *laboratory study* will help meet one of your needs, namely, that any backup system considered must offer a realistic promise of reliability and cost savings. The *full-scale production run* will assure you and your management in advance that, by using the Quantum System, your product can be made reliably to your standards or better.

If you agree to purchase the Quantum System provided we can demonstrate successful performance, please ship ingredient samples for delivery to me by next Friday. I will call you Wednesday to confirm details.

Cordially,

John H. Shorter

---

audience. Another way is to talk to people who have been involved in similar experiences to get their impressions, feelings,
and reactions.

Suppose, for example, that you are in the insurance business. You have an idea that sellers of homes, both individual
owners and realtors, would like to insure themselves against re-
course by buyers who, after closing and occupancy, discover un-
disclosed faults in the property. Your idea is to market to sellers
of homes a policy that would cover claims up to about $25,000.
The price of the policy would be about $300. You are not sure of
the reaction of actual prospects. Neither do you know exactly
how such a policy should be structured to appeal to both parties.
To become empathic, all you need do is talk to people who have
been through the experience. You will find out whether your
idea would have met their needs and, if so, whether they would
have bought it at the time. The strategy is not foolproof because
you are still not communicating with an actual audience, but
you have at least established some valuable parameters.

Pretend now that you are Harold S. Culkane, a vice president of a large, internationally known advertising agency. You
are in charge of new business. This means that you are always
on the lookout for major advertisers who wish to change their
ad agency. Identifying prospects is easy. Many large advertisers
who want to make a change send out what are known as
agency-selection questionnaires. These go to about twenty-five
leading agencies. You get twelve to fifteen such questionnaires
each year. Those agencies interested are asked to fill out the
questionnaire and submit it by a certain date. Each completed
questionnaire turns out to be a large document about an inch
thick. Most agencies respond. Thus the advertiser winds up with
a daunting pile of paper about a foot tall from which to make a
preliminary selection.

An advertiser, having sent out such a questionnaire, refuses
to meet with candidates until after it has made a "cut." Then it
sets up preliminary meetings with three or four candidate agencies that it likes the best, based on the information supplied in
the questionnaire. This protocol ties your hands. You know from
experience that unless you can get through the door, you have
no chance to solicit the business. This way you must depend

on someone's evaluation of your completed questionnaire. It is almost a lottery. This is not good enough for an aggressive new-business person like you. You must find a way to get to the prospective client before your competition does. You know from past experience that the first agency there has an odds-on advantage.

So how do you do this? You practice empathy. You imagine what is going through the minds of those responsible for hiring a new agency. Ad agency selection is an important task for all major advertisers because their sales volume is often linked directly to the effectiveness of their advertising. Knowing the needs of the people responsible for agency selection is fairly easy for you because you have made an exhaustive study of the matter. You have a presentation ready to educate any advertiser on the subject of selecting an agency. It provides reliable guidelines for the selection process and simplifies the task for any advertiser contemplating a change.

As soon as you have returned the requested agency-selection questionnaire, you identify the key person in the client organization and send off a proposal aimed at getting you and the prospective client face to face before your competitors know what is happening (see Figure 16-2).

This proposal is both a winner and a loser, depending on how you count your marbles. It wins only 30 percent of the time. The fact that it loses 70 percent of the time may make you decide that it is not very effective. Not so from Harold Culkane's viewpoint. Before he devised this approach, he was merely in the "lottery" and had no advantage, no way to get to prospective clients ahead of the competition. This way, three out of ten times Culkane gets there first. It pays off not only because his approach is persuasive but because his presentation is excellent and very helpful to most advertisers who see it. It goes without saying that WORLDWIDE is a perceptive and competent organization.

Advisory: (1) There is no substitute for careful, painstaking preparation. In some cases the word "overkill" describes the process. (2) Don't be discouraged by failure. Success is based on it. The very

Figure 16-2. Proposal for meeting with a prospective client.

Harold S. Culkane
WORLDWIDE Advertising
91 East 50th Street
New York, New York 10022

Mr. James H. Stockton
AMERICAN CONSUMER PRODUCTS, INC.
500 Fifth Avenue
New York, NY 10016

Dear Mr. Stockton:

Your agency-selection questionnaire has been completed and delivered to your office. Thank you for including us among the agencies you are considering.

Here are a few comments that may save you time and ease your decision-making process. At this point, as you receive volumes of information from many agencies, you may be asking questions such as:

- How can I digest the agency-selection questionnaires quickly?
- What are the best ways to compare the agencies?
- How should I establish measurable criteria?
- How should I make the first, second, and third cuts, etc.?

Most advertisers in your position want to make the change as soon as possible. If these thoughts represent your needs even in a general way, there are shortcuts available.

I suggest that you review agency-selection methods that are used successfully by other advertisers. Let me tell you how this could work out.

During a one-hour meeting, I will show you ten unbiased standards you can apply to any agency. These distill the experience of advertisers (not agencies). Clients and nonclients have told us about their bad decisions and how to avoid them. They have shared their good decisions and how to repeat them. It's a road map we offer you without obligation and without "commercials." Our agency will not be discussed at this meeting.

Results: This information can save you time and increase your chances of making the right decision. Panacea? No. Just excellent guidelines for you to apply in your own way. What's in it for us? Maybe nothing. You may apply these standards and select another agency. Then again, you may not.

If you agree to the meeting, I suggest August 27th or 28th. I'll call next Monday. If you are unavailable, please let your secretary know what time suits.

Cordially,

Harold S. Culkane
WORLDWIDE ADVERTISING

**best persuaders lose sometimes, but they learn all
the time.**

In summary, skillful persuaders will tell you that their experiences range from absolutely smooth, piece-of-cake efforts to
the roughest, toughest, most mind-boggling episodes imagin-
able. People who travel this route in life without benefit of the
kind of training you have gained from this book or in our seminar-workshops will find the task overwhelming. Those who
learn the basics and practice their persuasion skills will develop
enormous personal power and great success.

17

Can You Find the Errors?

Over the years, we have presented *The Anatomy of Persuasion* seminars in two formats. One is in a single session, one day or less, in which we cover only the fundamentals. The other format requires two half-day sessions back to back, with a one-hour overnight assignment. In the latter, people come to the seminar with an actual proposal subject of their own choosing in mind and already researched. (Participants receive guidance in advance on how to prepare.) This way the training given is customized to the exact needs of each participant.

After learning the fundamentals in the first session, participants go through a development process. They complete overnight assignments in which they prepare their actual proposals. Using the Outline Guide, they apply their own information to *The Anatomy of Persuasion* structure. The next day, in a workshop, each person presents the work to the group for analysis and constructive criticism. Thus each person gains practice in thinking through and discussing the proposals of the others in the group. The experience demonstrates the versatility of the process, that it works on any kind of persuasion task on any subject. Thus, participants leave the workshop with actual proposals ready for delivery and immediate action in the real world. This technique converts learning time into productive time. And many participants report immediate success with their first proposals.

To go through a similar experience, imagine that you are a participant in one of our workshops. You know the fundamentals. You are listening to a fellow participant, Bob Cousins, as he presents his proposal. Cousins is president of the ABC Company. As you listen to him, you sense a structural fault, but you can't quite identify it yet. We can tell you now that your instincts are on track. There *is* a fault here. Your task is to find it and to suggest to Cousins how he might fix it by editing his proposal.

Incidentally, in real life most proposals are made orally in face-to-face situations rather than in written form. However, the structure of such messages is the same regardless of the mode of delivery. In this book, written renditions of proposals are used, either in the form of letters or interoffice memos, as in this chapter.

Exercise 1: "More Technology"

Background

ABC Company is a consulting engineering firm. The field is overcrowded. Fierce price competition has sapped earnings. Some well-known firms have already gone under. Had ABC depended on selling standard engineering services alone, it too would have failed by now. Fortunately, ABC has survived because it has proprietary technology to sell in combination with its regular engineering services.

So far, this combination has given ABC a substantial edge over competitors. For example, if a company wants to convert an available agricultural product to high-quality ethyl alcohol at low cost, ABC can provide the technology to do this. ABC's engineering service can also customize the final design, prepare the location, install the unit, start it up, all in compliance with environmental regulations. Thus the company offers a "turn-key" product and service guaranteed to work exactly as represented.

If ABC's success is to continue, more new marketable technology must be found to "package" with its engineering services. A company called TELCOM appears to have the kind of technology that would fit with ABC's market. Cousins believes that the acquisition of TELCOM *might* fill the need for more technology.

But before making a final decision and recommendation, Cousins says he wants to investigate TELCOM in much greater depth. On a matter as important as this, he feels he should get the agreement of his boss, Dick Swope, who is CEO of ABC. To do this he defined his audience, wrote his objective, and prepared his proposal in memo form (see Figure 17-1). Here's how the first two items went:

AUDIENCE
Dick Swope, CEO of the ABC Company

OBJECTIVE
To get Swope's approval for a study to acquire
TELCOM*

Comments and Opinions

On the face of it, Bob Cousins's work seems okay. He used *The Anatomy of Persuasion* structure; he ended with a request for specific action by a specific time and so on. Yet there is something about the proposal that does not seem to work. As someone once said, "If it doesn't jell, it isn't aspic."

We get a clue from Cousins's PLAN, which appears to be a misstatement. It suggests—wrongly, I believe—that Cousins views TELCOM as a prime candidate for acquisition. Yet Cousins stated in the workshop only that he wanted to investigate that possibility. He has not yet made a final decision. Cousins really means that TELCOM, as of now, should be a candidate for evaluation. This tells us that we should look at Cousins's OBJECTIVE. When we do, we find the root of the problem. The PLAN statement is out of whack because the OBJECTIVE is faulty.

He worded his OBJECTIVE ambiguously. What Cousins wants to do is to get official approval to study TELCOM in depth, and that is all. The operative misleading words here are "for a study to acquire TELCOM." Cousins needs to make his OBJECTIVE statement more specific. It is clear now that Cousins

---

*Remember, AUDIENCE and OBJECTIVE are not part of the finished proposal. Cousins's audience, Dick Swope, does not see the written objective because it is not included in the proposal.

Figure 17-1. Example of a flawed proposal.

MEMORANDUM

To: Richard A. Swope—CEO, ABC Company

From: Robert B. Cousins—President, ABC Company

Subject: TELECOM Incorporated

NEEDS*

One of ABC's goals is to grow by broadening the markets for its product. This growth has been achieved by using the proprietary technology we have now and by adding more through acquisitions.

PLAN

ABC proposes TELCOM as a prime candidate for acquisition.

HOW-IT-WORKS

TELCOM offers several features that make it worthy.

1. Like ABC, TELCOM is a service-oriented company.
2. TELCOM would provide ABC with technological enhancements because most of TELCOM's areas of expertise complement those of ABC.
3. TELCOM's strong position in telecommunication hardware and software offers needed diversification.

RESULTS

The purchase of TELCOM would provide an 18 percent return on investment, double the potential for ABC in current markets, and add the diversification necessary for future growth. This combination would help ABC expand the profitability of standard engineering services through "packaging" with proprietary technology.

NEXT STEP

I request a meeting with you to discuss this potential opportunity. I'll call you Monday to find a convenient time.

PLEASE STOP HERE.
CONTINUE READING AFTER YOU HAVE FINISHED EDITING.

*The structural indicators (NEEDS, PLAN, HOW-IT-WORKS, RESULTS, and NEXT STEP) are added for convenient reference only. In an actual proposal these indicators would not be included.

really wants to look before he leaps. He wants Swope to approve a study of TELCOM to help them decide whether or not ABC should acquire TELCOM.

Now we can see how seriously flawed this proposal really is. The PLAN proposes "TELCOM as a prime candidate for acquisition" and ignores the idea of a preliminary study. The HOW-IT-WORKS contains information about the strengths that TELCOM would bring to ABC and nothing about how the study would be carried out, or even, in the case of the faulty PLAN, how the acquisition would be consummated.

TELCOM's strengths are really supporting evidence that Cousins must provide so that Swope can appreciate the potential value of the study being proposed. This kind of supporting evidence, if lengthy, might be attached to the proposal or, if brief as in this case, be included in the HOW-IT-WORKS part. *A key point:* Please note how a carelessly written OBJECTIVE has resulted in Cousins preparing an aimless, drifting proposal that Swope could easily regard as confusing or reject altogether as precipitous.

Having recognized his errors, Cousins rewrote his OBJECTIVE as follows:

NEW OBJECTIVE
To get approval to study the possible acquisition of
TELCOM.

Armed with a more precise OBJECTIVE, Cousins prepared a new proposal. As you will see in Figure 17-2, the changes were significant throughout.

> **Advisory:** *Fuzzy thinking can quickly derail an otherwise effective proposal.* **This one was selected to illustrate how "little things," such as a careless OBJECTIVE and a PLAN that is out of whack with the author's intentions, can make the difference between a crisp, effective communication and one that is seriously lacking in clarity and ineffective in purpose.**

Once again, be sure you get your OBJECTIVE right in the first place because this is your message to you about what you want

Figure 17-2. Revised proposal repairing faulty plan and providing HOW-IT-WORKS steps.

MEMORANDUM

To: Richard A. Swope—CEO, ABC Company
From: Robert B. Cousins—President, ABC Company
Subject: TELCOM Incorporated

NEEDS:

One of ABC's goals is to grow by broadening the markets for its products and services. As you know, this growth is achieved with the proprietary technology we have acquired. Our current need is to add more technology through acquisitions.

PLAN:

I propose that you authorize a study of TELCOM as a possible candidate for acquisition.

HOW-IT-WORKS:

The study would include:

1. A review of available technology and of the financial condition of TELCOM
2. An evaluation of the new business opportunities that a merger of the two companies would create.
3. A five-year business plan for the two companies, if merged
4. One-year and five-year sales and earnings forecasts
5. A cost of $60,000 and two months to complete

TELCOM is a prime candidate because:

1. Like ABC, TELCOM is a service-oriented company.
2. TELCOM probably could provide ABC with needed technological enhancements because most of TELCOM's areas of expertise complement those of ABC.
3. TELCOM's strong position in telecommunication hardware and software may provide ABC with needed diversification.

RESULTS:

• If the evaluation verifies current impressions, acquisition of TELCOM should double the potential for ABC in current markets and add the diversification necessary for future growth.

• This combination would help ABC expand the profitability of standard engineering services through continued "packaging" with proprietary technology.

• The proposed evaluation of TELCOM will provide ABC with a clear definition of the opportunity an acquisition would, or would not, provide.

NEXT STEP:

I request your approval in principle and a meeting to discuss the details of implementation. I'll call you Monday to find a convenient time.

to accomplish with *this* proposal. After doing that, be sure your PLAN and NEXT STEP align with your OBJECTIVE and let your HOW-IT-WORKS explain how the PLAN will be carried out.

Exercise 2: "The Merger Crunch"

Charlie Gordon is in one of our seminar-workshops. It is the second day, and each participant is presenting a proposal. Charlie has prepared a proposal to present to Harry Howard, CEO of Company A. Charlie is vice president of human resources at Company A, which is about to acquire a major competitor, Company B. The acquisition will make the new company dominant in its industry.

Background

Between the two companies there is much duplication of product, function, service, and personnel. Everyone involved knows that jobs will be eliminated as a result of this jolting consolidation. For example, the new company will need only one director of accounting, one legal department, and so on. Charlie himself is nervous because the new company will need only one VP for human resources. Harry Howard, as CEO of Company A, will be forced to slash middle- and top-management jobs. Charlie is working directly with Harry on this task. Charlie and Harry estimate that the forthcoming cuts will bring the number of management people from a current 600 down to 400.

Matching the best people to the appropriate jobs is critical, risky, and time-consuming, especially when each of the two top management teams has serious blind spots. Neither group knows the people in the other. Loyalty clouds objectivity. Yet logic says that the most effective alignment of personnel should involve the most talented people from each company. Gloom and tension prevail.

Obviously Harry Howard wants to select and keep the most talented people in each company and dump the others. Making an unbiased selection presents problems. One problem is identifying the best people in Company B. Another problem is time—or the lack of it. Charlie and Harry know that the people they most want to keep will be the hardest to hold. These, the most competent, aggressive, and self-confident people in each company, will refuse to tolerate uncertainty for very long. Both men are aware that the copy machines are cranking out résumés by the ream and that headhunters already are reconnoitering like hawks over roadkill.

Therefore, Harry has asked Charlie to come up with a plausible program to delay decisions on these key people until the selection process can be completed. Harry believes that "most people would rather stay than go if all things are equal." Charlie believes that Harry really wants a delaying tactic to dangle real or imagined carrots in front of everyone to restore optimism until the moment of truth arrives and the ax finally falls.

Charlie has an idea that might do the job. It is called the Performance Profile Program (PPP). You, as an imaginary member of the seminar-workshop, are about to review the proposal (see Figure 17-3) that Charlie developed for Harry. This is how he wrote up the two items meant for himself:

AUDIENCE
Harry Howard, CEO of Company A, is analytical, logical, and political. He has the power to make this decision and move ahead on his own.

OBJECTIVE
To obtain Harry's approval to use the Performance Profile Program (PPP) as the personnel-selection tool.

Comments and Opinions

If you believe there is a misalignment here, you're right. The fault is in the first alignment. Assuming that Charlie's OBJECTIVE and PLAN are okay, his failure to ask Harry for a specific action in his NEXT STEP is glaring. Instead of asking Harry to approve the PPP idea, Charlie has asked Harry for a meeting. While there is nothing wrong with trying to persuade a busy CEO to schedule a meeting, if a meeting was what Charlie wanted to propose, his OBJECTIVE should have stated as much. It didn't.

Figure 17-3. Proposal for reallocating personnel following a new acquisition.

MEMORANDUM

To: Harry J. Howard

From: Charles Q. Gordon

Subject: Reallocation of Personnel

NEEDS

Your needs, as I understand them, are: (1) to define and describe the management-level jobs needed to operate the new company efficiently, and (2) to identify the most qualified management people in each company to fill those jobs.

PLAN

Proposed: the Performance Profile Program (PPP) as a means for satisfying both needs.

HOW-IT-WORKS

PPP defines both operational and staff functions that are needed to operate the new company.

PPP also describes each management-level job in terms of the skills, knowledge, and experience required by the incumbent.

Finally, PPP can be prioritized; jobs for which matching is most critical come first, etc. (both companies).

PPP can be in full operation in ninety days, with first-priority jobs handled in thirty days. The management consulting firm Smith & Jones developed this program and will supervise its installation. The fee is $140,000, complete. Their client list is attached.

RESULTS

PPP will speed the process of matching people with jobs and thereby reduce the number of defections by desirable candidates.

It will also reduce the number of job-match mistakes even though all our decision-making people are strangers to at least half the candidates for any given job.

It fits our timing needs and is affordable.

NEXT STEP

I request a thirty-minute meeting to map out the major elements and priorities. I'll ask your assistant to schedule a mutually convenient time for the proposed meeting.

So, after developing an otherwise good proposal, one that should sell Harry on PPP, Charlie has committed what could be a fatal error by not "asking for the order." When that was pointed out to him, Charlie explained that he had hesitated to put this request on the line because he thought asking straight-out for approval of something as complex as PPP might be too much to expect of a single-page proposal.

We took exception, because many major deals have been consummated via brief, well-conceived proposals. Other than that, Charlie did a good job with this proposal. He covered all the bases, followed the logic, and presented excellent benefits in the RESULTS section. On top of that he produced a concise, easy-to-read, single-page proposal. But Charlie still worried that Harry would want to know much more about PPP before he approved. Because Charlie knows Harry and we don't, we suggested that he change his NEXT STEP by asking Harry for *approval in principle* of PPP and then offering a meeting to handle any questions Harry might have. Charlie's revision came out as follows:

CHARLIE'S NEW NEXT STEP
Therefore, as next steps, I request (1) *your approval of the PPP idea in principle* and (2) a thirty-minute meeting to map out the major elements and priorities. I'll ask your assistant to schedule a mutually convenient time for the proposed meeting.

Advisory: *Don't fail to ask for the action you want.* Salespeople are *supposed* to know a lot about persuasion, but if there is one basic fault among them, it is a failure to ask for the order. If you don't believe this, just ask the next few sales managers you meet. This fault is not confined to salespeople. Most of us hesitate before we finally ask for a specific action after we have proposed something—possibly from fear of rejection and the consequent pain of embarrassment that follows turndowns. The only answer is to just bull your way through. The worst anyone can do to you is to say no.

Exercise 3: "Supervising the Supervisors"

Background

Auditing is a basic service offered by certified public accounting firms. For larger firms, fees for audits represent 40 to 60 percent of their annual gross. But this segment of the business is declining because auditing has become a commodity service. An audit is an audit when done by any competent CPA firm. Large firms with many offices and larger overhead are being squeezed out of the auditing business by smaller firms with lower overhead. Some clients have discovered that it is not always cost-effective to engage a large firm unless a prestigious name is needed as decoration for the company's annual report. Worse, to the dismay of larger CPA firms, smaller ones sometimes discount audit services to open doors. This creates a serious marketing problem for large firms.

Jeff Leary, a senior managing partner of a large firm, has a solution in mind. It's a two-part marketing thrust. One part is to diversify into nontraditional services such as specialized management consulting. Establishing something new takes time, however. The second part is to buy the needed time by slowing the decay of the auditing business until new consulting services are in place and profitable. To do this, Leary needs to tighten auditing procedures to make them more efficient, more competitive, and more profitable.

Leary knows that many field managers, namely the partners in charge (PICs) of the firm's many offices, have themselves delegated audits to supervisory personnel. In short, the PICs are not paying enough attention to their overall responsibilities, and discipline has slackened. Leary's task is to persuade PICs to refocus their supervisory attention on shaping up the employees who are doing the audits. But he does not want them to neglect their other work in the process.

This is how Leary defined his audience and the objective of his proposal (given in Figure 17-4):

AUDIENCE

PICs of the field offices whose responsibility it is to manage the business efficiently and return a substan-

Figure 17-4. Proposal to increase efficiency of a large firm's audit services.

MEMORANDUM

To: Partners-in-Charge—All Offices

From: Jeff Leary

Subject: Audit Business

NEEDS

In response to pressures to reduce our fees, we need to devise ways to remain competitive, deliver high-quality audits, and yet maintain our profitability. As management people, we all face time pressures and the need to increase our efficiency. We also need to train personnel on the job while at the same time keeping any additional load on our schedule to a minimum.

PLAN

I propose that you temporarily increase your personal supervision of audit-team planning.

HOW-IT-WORKS

Let me suggest a method used successfully by one of our PICs. She reviews prior-year papers before each audit team begins planning (10 minutes). She focuses on auditing and documentation methods and prepares a partial list of apparent inefficiencies. She reviews these with the auditor-in-charge (AIC) as first-glance examples of inefficiencies. At the AIC's first planning meeting, she requests that a search for more inefficiencies be made (10 minutes).

After the AIC's team has prepared an audit plan, a final planning meeting is held. She attends to explain why special attention is needed. She emphasizes the problem of competitive pressures and the need for efficiency (10 minutes). This PIC spends one-half hour per audit on this important remedial work.

RESULTS

Her payoff was prompt. Earnings were maintained while audit fees were reduced. Team time spent on adults was reduced 30 percent in the first six months. Further savings were achieved in the next six months but without continued management attention. Management time was leveraged as AICs learned the value of careful planning.

NEXT STEP

Please read the attached details of the case mentioned above. Then look over the audit-planning materials enclosed. We request that you use these on your next audit engagement and that you report your results by June 1st.

tial profit for the firm. Each of these people, like the captain of a ship, operates independently of higher authority most of the time.

OBJECTIVE

To get PICs to improve the efficiency of audit services.

Comments and Opinions

We know that Jeff Leary's long-term objective is to solve a marketing problem. We know that he must maintain earnings during a period of transition. So, did he lose that perspective when he constructed this proposal? No. Did he fog the "big picture"? No.

Each PIC, having earnings responsibility, faces the same marketing problem locally as Jeff does nationally. Therefore, isn't the real need to make the transition from one type of business to another? No. And since tightening up on audit procedures, though mandatory, is only one part of the task, has Jeff misstated his real objective? No.

When developing an OBJECTIVE for a proposal, remember that you are thinking of *immediate* action, in other words, what you want to accomplish with *this* proposal. No long-term thinking is needed here. Jeff was not trying to persuade the PICs to participate in his two-part marketing thrust. He was not even telling them about it in this communication. All he wants to do is persuade PICs to improve the efficiency of their audit services. We think Jeff did that with this proposal. Therefore, we don't find any structural fault in his work.

Summary

In summary, some proposals are simple and clear-cut. Others become frightfully and unnecessarily complicated through the misstatement of the objective or the misalignment of the different parts of the proposal. Usually the inexperienced person produces the latter. The best, most effective messages follow a logical course and mesh with the thought process of the buying mind. When done effectively, a proposal is a concise, honest communication that seems to get the desired result with the ease of a professional athlete in action. Remember, persuasion is a process. Keep it as simple and straightforward as you can.

18

Selling Your Ideas to Higher Management

Most people who are part of an organization will tell you that one of their most difficult tasks is getting acceptance for their ideas from higher management. Even professional salespeople, those trained to sell products or services to outside customers, agree that selling their own ideas within their organizations is usually much harder than their regular selling work. Yet, although "internal selling" is difficult for most people, an anointed few seem to breeze through and get acceptance time after time. Why?

Obstacles

To answer that question, it is first necessary to analyze the task you face, paying particular attention to the obstacles, especially when several layers of management are involved.

Remember that like Cassandra, "a prophet is without honor in his own house."

As an insider, the odds can be against you in at least two ways. The people you must persuade are fully aware of your shortcomings and at the same time totally blind to their own prejudices. By contrast, people from outside the organization, coming with the status of consultants and honored guests, gain the undivided attention of the big boss. Their "wisdom," whatever its quality, is worth whatever price the boss is paying for it. These people last until their warts become visible through the glitz or until their lack of talent betrays them. Unfortunately for some of us insiders, these unwelcome interlopers sometimes add much needed value and turn out to be worthy of their high fees in spite of what we think of them.

You often lack knowledge of the internal competition.

On the outside you usually know your competitors. But on the inside others in your organization may be generating ideas that you know nothing about just as you are generating ideas that others know nothing about. Although another's seemingly unrelated proposal may not appear as competition, it may compete directly for the limited amount of management time and money available. Many otherwise excellent projects have come a cropper because someone else got the ear of management first. There were just not enough resources for two projects. Unless you have cased the joint carefully, you are unlikely to know about this potential conflict. The only thing you can do is to hone your proposal the best you can, get there ASAP, and hope that the others wind up in the boondocks. Take your first-aid kit, because you are not going to win them all.

Do not fall in love with ideas, especially your own.

We all fall in love with ideas, just as we do with our children and pets. When we do, our biases destroy objectivity, distort perspective, enhance rationalizing, test honesty, and set us up for narcissistic failure. Consider the following love story.

When Antifreeze Met Reality

Several years ago, during a market share battle between two manufacturers of permanent automotive antifreeze, the marketing people at ABC Corporation came up with a new product idea. The product was to be a *two-year antifreeze*, that is, guaranteed for two years instead of for one, as with the current anti-freeze product.

Antifreeze is what keeps your car's cooling system from freezing in winter. The name *permanent* was given to antifreeze made with ethylene glycol because it does not boil away as did the alcohol-based antifreezes used previously. Motorists liked the care-free benefit of permanent antifreeze.

In time, some motorists discovered that permanent anti-freeze worked well as a year-round coolant. Furthermore, they discovered that one change would last several years. Each anti-freeze manufacturer, alarmed that the market would shrink, responded with publicity campaigns to correct this "misuse." Every fall, cautions about how antifreeze should be replaced each year appeared in the media. The message was that old anti-freeze would turn bad and cause costly rust and corrosion damage to cooling systems. (If, technically, there was validity to this warning, it probably was a stretch.)

After several years of such propaganda, the antifreeze marketers at ABC came to believe their own publicity. By now the ABC people were positive that antifreeze was perceived as a one-year product by motorists. They reasoned that perception, not behavior, was the important thing. The fact that many motorists used the antifreeze year-round without ill effects was simply ignored. Ergo, the new *two-year antifreeze* certainly would be hailed in the marketplace as a significant product improvement.

How they got funding approval from top management remains a mystery, except that "love conquers all." The launch was staged, complete with a national advertising campaign. You guessed it, the *two-year antifreeze* fizzled like a ten-cent rocket on the Fourth of July.*

Add to this fiasco the Edsel and New Coke flops, Sony's Betamax, 3-D movies, and aluminum wiring to remind yourself that love is just as blind in commerce as it is anywhere else.

---

*Incidentally, the task of tracking down and placing blame for something like this in large corporations can baffle the likes of Sherlock Holmes and absolutely flummox the FBI.

You may lack knowledge of the real needs of management.

Gaining clear knowledge of the needs of the organization as the decision makers view them is sometimes difficult to accomplish unless you happen to be one of them. Decision makers often fail to express their needs clearly. (Or we, down below, need hearing aids.)

Recently, we met a biochemist who was searching for a new drug. His project was failing because he was on the wrong research path. Consequently, he wanted to change the direction of his research. Unfortunately, he was unable to get approval from his "stubborn" management. In desperation, he attended *The Anatomy of Persuasion* seminar. Two weeks later, using a new approach learned with us, he got approval to change direction. We asked what he did that was different. He said that instead of talking in terms of his needs as he had before, he finally figured out what his management's needs were and addressed them in those terms. That did the trick.

What now? In the most simple terms, here is what you do. Start by getting a clear, verified idea of management's needs as management views them and not as you view them. Don't guess. Get it straight. Get it right. Then set about proposing well-thought-out ideas designed to fill those needs effectively. It is not easy, but that is all there is to it in principle.

Take care when you interpret messages from your management.

Carl is one of our clients. As president of his company, he said he wanted to stimulate creativity among his marketing people. At his request, we arranged for a seminar on creativity. To end the event with a flare, we asked Carl to wind up the session with a few supporting words of wisdom. His pontifications sounded good to us. But his message came across differently to one vice president, who whispered, "Carl will like any idea as long as it is his." Perhaps Carl was misunderstood. We thought he was trying to focus the creative thinking of his people on ideas relevant to a particular part of the business because he did not want to deal with suggestions that didn't pertain to the immediate task. But we are not sure what Carl meant. We doubt that the vice president was right. If we worked for Carl as employees, we certainly would find a way to be sure of how he saw his needs.

If you can't decode the messages, you may be DOA.

A few people in every organization master the internal selling process. Others fall short. Tom's experience is a case in point.

As a bright, ambitious person, Tom has a responsible, middle-management marketing job in a large corporation. He earns a respectable income. He described his futile efforts to get his management to buy into a promising, low-risk business venture. His idea revived unused technology. An alert research man tweaked this technology and came up with a viable and innovative product idea that could fit neatly into the current product line and be sold profitably by the current sales force with minimum extra effort. The new product idea promised a handsome return on a relatively small investment of $1 million, which is not much for this company.

Tom and the research man had conducted successful field trials. Prospective customers were enthusiastic and signed tentative purchasing agreements. The business promised a return of the initial investment in two years. After that the business would produce annual pretax earnings of $1.5 million with an expected life cycle of ten years.

Tom said he had made two proposals to top management. After each he was asked to put the project on hold. At this point, Tom sensed he was becoming an irritant and could be verging on career damage. Just as he was about to drop the matter, he got a brush-off response saying that his proposal didn't fit the "long-range vision" of the company.

Neither Tom nor his associates had ever heard of any corporate "vision." Tom was angry. He felt that management owed him more than the vague, even phony, reason given for the rejection. He felt that they should have made their decision after the first presentation and not held him and others in the organization on tenterhooks for several months.

To Tom, his management was clearly duplicitous: "They say they want ideas and suggestions, and then they abuse those who submit them." Tom isn't the first to fail when trying to sell an idea within one's own organization. And he will not be the last. One thing is sure, Tom will think more than twice before working his head off again "for the good of the company." Another thing is sure, Tom should spend more time studying the needs of his management before giving unsolicited advice about running the business.

Before we leave Tom, try a riddle: What is worse than a piece of unsolicited advice? Answer: Two pieces of unsolicited advice. Sometimes people like Tom don't know how to decode messages from above. Worse, some accept the literal meaning without a second thought.

Understand that your path can be long and hazardous.

Any given internal project may have to go through several levels of approval. Several yeses may be needed to succeed, but only one no along the line can, and usually will, kill your proposal. Sometimes your opposition within the organization is invisible. Like Tom, you may never find out who hexed your proposal or why. So, one good way of selling up the organization is to use a carefully constructed, step-by-step plan.

Overcoming the Obstacles

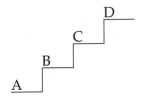

Let's say you are A, and that you have a proposal that requires top-management approval. To get that, you must persuade D, who is three steps above your level. And you know that going directly to D is completely out of the question.

So, to get all the way up to D, you must at least get nonobjection from your immediate boss, who is B, and from her boss, who is C.

Start by carefully preparing a proposal to D. Do it just as though you had direct access to D. Go through the whole exercise—AUDIENCE, OBJECTIVE, PLAN, HOW-IT-WORKS, RESULTS, and NEXT STEP. This becomes your basic proposal because it will help you describe to B and C exactly what you want to accomplish with D. Remember, end runs around management are not prudent no matter what the sign on the door may say. So don't send your proposal along to D just yet. Hold it until you get the required help from B and C.

As your second step, prepare another proposal. This one is to B. As part of it, you will use your basic proposal to describe to B exactly what you want to accomplish with D. The OBJECTIVE of this second proposal is to get B to buy into the idea you wish to propose to D *and* to help you sell C on helping you get to D. Having your basic proposal to D in hand is a vital element at this juncture. B and C will need to know exactly what they are being asked to endorse and what action is required of them. If your basic proposal reveals weakness of any kind, or if it should incorporate suggestions from B or C, stop promptly and fix it.

When you are ready to prepare your proposal to B, you will notice that even though the basic idea (what you wish to sell to D) is the same, almost everything else about the proposal changes.

Your AUDIENCE is different, B instead of D.

Your OBJECTIVE with B also is different. Granted, you want B to buy into the same basic idea, but there is another equally important part. You also want B to agree to help you get C to not only buy into the basic idea but also to agree to help you (and B) to carry it on upward to finally persuade D.

The NEEDS part of this proposal is different. B is a different person in a different place in the organization with a different job, different viewpoint, different responsibilities, different relationships, and so on. You should be quite familiar with B's needs because B is your immediate boss.

The PLAN statement for the proposal to B is different because the OBJECTIVE is different from that of your basic proposal to D. However you decide to word it, you are asking B to do two things instead of one—buy into the basic idea *and also* help sell it to C.

The HOW-IT-WORKS is different because the PLAN is different. You may decide to include some reference to your basic proposal to D here to show what is involved.

The RESULTS (benefits) are different because they reflect B's needs and not those of D.

The NEXT STEP is also different because the action you want B to take derives from the OBJECTIVE, which is different. And that's it. You have completed your proposal to B.

The next proposal in this series is from B to C. I suggest that you hold off on this one until you have B sold and ready to help you proceed. When you start to build that proposal, remember that you must recheck each step for the differences, starting with AUDIENCE, and go on from there just as you did with the proposal from you to B.

This all may sound overly complicated and nitpicky, but it really is not. This approach will help keep you on track. Selling up the organization is difficult at best and even more so without a reliable guideline. Take it on faith; this is a tested approach. It will work and also remove much, but not all, of the frustration from what otherwise can be an onerous task.

You will reconfirm this advice through both good and bad experiences. A good experience is when you find a flaw in your proposal and fix it before you present it. A bad experience is when someone else finds a flaw in your proposal as you are giving it. The latter case is usually more memorable.

Again, basic and critical to the entire process is the first proposal, A to D. Take extra time at the start to create it and to refine it en route, and the rest of your work should follow along without too much complication. With practice you will know not only just what you are doing but also specifically, precisely, and accurately how you will do it. Your confidence will build as your expertise is validated.

There is no reason why you should not be among those anointed few who breeze through by mastering the art of internal selling. Remember, the person at the top uses the same process for making a buying decision that you do: NEEDS, RECOGNITION, SEARCH, EVALUATION, and DECISION. Develop your skills to mesh with that, and you are the winner.

19

The Anatomy of Persuasion as a Management Tool

When experienced managers need the best problem-solving ideas their people can deliver, they generally seek ideas that are logical, innovative, soundly researched, and, above all, ideas that call for specific action. Such results require disciplined thinking from each member of the group. Each person must think and communicate using logic and language that the others can understand. Liken this management process to conducting an orchestra. Each player must be able to perform competently alone. The conductor, having set the objective by selecting the music, leads the members in concert to make the whole greater than the sum of its parts. Would that it were so with all management undertakings.

Now that you have come this far in the book, you can see how a group of individuals practiced in *The Anatomy of Persuasion* thinking process has the discipline required to develop and propose ideas that meet objectives set by their manager. When these people come together as a group, each with a proposal, synergistic power is possible. In orderly discussion, members quickly separate logic from emotion; they temper personal enthusiasm with realism without inhibiting creativity; they refine ideas and propose needed action. For managers, there is a bonus benefit: a management tool that can be used time after time whenever the need arises.

A case in point is the experience of Phillip L. Pennartz, who headed a new company and used *The Anatomy of Persuasion* as a management tool to move it along. The new company, called Procomp, was a joint venture between a Swedish company and DuPont. The Swedish company contributed technology to increase the output of paper mills; DuPont contributed its marketing and technical presence in the American paper industry. Phil's comments tell the story best:

> *The Anatomy of Persuasion* training was a key element in making two essential things happen at Procomp when I was president.
>
> One of these was to unify twenty-five strangers into a cooperative working force that was capable of functioning in the highly competitive environment of the U.S. paper industry. This joint venture between the DuPont Company and Eka Nobel, our Swedish partner, required us to assemble a staff of technical, sales, and marketing people from the paper industry. We were able to get the people, but establishing trust and effective working relationships among strangers turned out to be a problem.
>
> The other was to find an effective way to integrate the people and their thinking to get a flow of useful, problem-solving ideas that would effectively address the tasks at hand. We wanted to help these people develop a unified and effective approach to the task of making and marketing our new products.
>
> Our people learned a thinking process that helped them analyze, organize, and get buy-in for our ideas, plans, and policies. As a group we learned how to sort good ideas from poor or marginal ideas. We were able to achieve continuous improvement, because everyone in the group understood the process. In summary, *The Anatomy of Persuasion* as a tool not only integrated the group, but it also showed us how to develop customer presentations that earned business. In all my travels I have never seen another program like it. Incidentally, many of these people tell me that we have given them a lifetime skill.

How can you make this work for you and your organization as a management tool to unify your people into a cooperative working force that is capable of functioning in a highly competitive environment? There are two phases. First, train your people in the process. Second, make the process one of your standard operational procedures.

Phase One: Training

I suggest that you start by expressing a need. It might go something like this:

> To be effective, our group needs to generate and propose ideas that meet our changing conditions. Because this is an ongoing task, we need to become better at identifying our best ideas and moving them from concept to application faster. It is also important that we all think and speak in the same terms just as we have settled on one operating system in our computers.

Once you have registered this need, your next step is to introduce *The Anatomy of Persuasion* as a candidate method and propose that the group learn the technique. You can present your own seminar-workshop using this book as your leader's guide. Or you can have each person read the book and then prepare and present a proposal to the group for critique.

If you decide to do this training yourself, you will be ready once you have developed a few proposals yourself. Your job will be easier with a partner who will learn and work along with you. There is nothing like having an educated sounding board for proposals. In this way you will sense the remarkable group dynamics that are possible when two or more people are interacting with this thinking process. If you decide that handling the training yourself is not appropriate, assign the task to one or two others.

The training should be continued until you decide that each person in your group is proficient. Most people develop skill more rapidly if they have the opportunity to critique proposals developed by other members of the group.

Once your people discover that the technique learned is an extremely valuable lifetime skill applicable to all phases of their lives, you will be surprised at how fast they will embrace it. To continue the training, ask each person to prepare and present two more proposals on work-related subjects. After no more than two such follow-up meetings, each person should be competent to think skillfully with this discipline. At this point, it is important that you announce that all future proposals should be presented in this format.

Phase Two: Working on Real Proposals

Now you are ready to put your group to work on a real task. To start, focus the group by defining both the problem and the objective in crystal-clear terms. Assure yourself that each participant understands exactly what you mean. As you have seen, flawed objectives are ruinous. Each participant should be reminded to screen his or her proposal in the early stages to be sure that it is in the ballpark and that it is tightly focused on the given problems and objective.

Your next step is to have each member present a proposal for group critique. As you lead, you will notice group dynamics build. Soon the group will start running itself. This happy state of affairs is the result of the discipline imparted by both the thinking process and your own clearly defined objective. You can expect the group to propose a well-defined course of action. And don't forget your bonus benefit: an established and successfully tested new management tool for ongoing use.

A Final Word: Thinking and Talking in Terms of Benefits

Benefits. That's what people buy. But a benefit to one person may not appeal to another. As you know, finding the operative benefit in any situation is the key to successful persuasion and personal satisfaction. You've finished *The Anatomy of Persuasion. SO WHAT?*

So your effectiveness will increase because you now know the fundamentals of the most powerful force in the world. *That's called persuasion. SO WHAT?*

So you know the thinking process people use when they make decisions to buy something. *That's called insight. SO WHAT?*

So you now have learned to concentrate your attention on the needs of other people. *That's called focused observation. SO WHAT?*

So, with the needs of others clearly in mind, you are able to define exactly what actions you want to propose. *That's called setting objectives. SO WHAT?*

So you know how to structure logical proposals that are specifically designed to meet needs and gain acceptance. *That's called skillful planning. SO WHAT?*

So you present a proposal and it's accepted. *That's called success. SO WHAT?*

So you do it again and again, because it works. Success breeds success, and your ability to influence "buying" minds continues to grow. *That's called a lot of success. SO WHAT?*

So, in time, people will start asking your advice on how they too can get the kind of results you achieve so effectively. *That's called leadership. SO WHAT?*

So, with the knowledge and opportunity you've gained from *The Anatomy of Persuasion*, there is only one thing you need do. *That's called practice.*

If you practice the principles you have learned from this book, you will attain a power of leadership far beyond that of most other people. Keep perspective. Always have another good, salable idea in your hip pocket and ready to go. Remember, the presence of a problem is often merely the absence of an idea.

Appendixes

Here, so you can find them easily, are *The Anatomy of Persuasion* tools you will be using from now on to prepare your persuasion tasks. Included are A Checklist of Common Errors, the Preparation Guidelines, the Outline Guide, and the Structure and Alignment Chart. Please feel free to make as many copies of these tools as you need for your personal use.

1

A Checklist of Common Errors

Now that you have learned and applied *The Anatomy of Persuasion* principles, you may be asked to critique persuasive material created by others. Or you may wish to give your own work a close, detailed look before presentation. To ease that task for you we have prepared a checklist of common errors. This will help you to pinpoint flaws and to give constructive criticism quickly and easily when asked. If you have acted on the suggestions in Chapter 15, Building Your Own Proposal, you will find this checklist valuable.

Some people don't like the idea of checklists. Their very existence suggests mental flaws in the person dependent on them. Preoccupation is a flaw in all of us.

I am reminded of the Naval Aviation cadet who did not like to use the checklists present in every aircraft. He had gone just far enough in his training to become overconfident. He was by now a "hot" pilot. One day he was flying solo and on final approach to a landing. Because he did not use his landing checklist, he forgot to lower his landing gear. Just as he crossed the airport boundary, two things happened simultaneously. The landing gear warning horn blew loudly as he cut his power, and the control tower operator, noticing the gear-up condition of the airplane, advised the cadet repeatedly and frantically by radio. In spite of these two blatant warnings, this "hot" pilot landed with the landing gear up, inflicting serious damage to the aircraft. When the commanding officer called this young man on the carpet to ask why he had not responded to the warning from the tower, he explained that the landing gear warning horn had made so much noise that he could not hear the radio.

After you have prepared your proposals, we suggest that you use the following checklist:

The Anatomy of Persuasion® *Checklist*

AUDIENCE

- ✓ Is your prospect the person (or group) who can act on your proposal?
- ✓ Are there others who might influence the decision-making process?

OBJECTIVE

- ✓ Does the OBJECTIVE state exactly what you want to accomplish with this particular proposal *and nothing more*?

NEEDS

- ✓ Are the NEEDS specifically those of your prospect?
- ✓ Are the NEEDS clearly stated?
- ✓ Have you quantified the NEEDS (time, cost, etc.)?
- ✓ Does the prospect agree that these are his/her NEEDS?
- ✓ Are there any other NEEDS of which your prospect is unaware or believes are already satisfied?

PLAN

- ✓ Does the PLAN statement derive logically from the OBJECTIVE?
- ✓ Does the PLAN state exactly what you want your prospect to do *and nothing more*?
- ✓ Will the PLAN, if accepted, achieve your OBJECTIVE?
- ✓ Have you quantified the PLAN (time, cost, people, etc.)?
- ✓ Have you included a transition line from PLAN to HIW?

HOW-IT-WORKS

- ✓ Does the HIW explain in principle how the PLAN will be carried out?

✓ Have you quantified and summarized the HIW (time, cost, people, etc.)?

RESULTS (BENEFITS)

✓ Are the BENEFITS expressed as BENEFITS rather than as *features*?
✓ Is there a BENEFIT for each NEED?
✓ Is each BENEFIT in the same sequence as the corresponding NEED?
✓ Are the BENEFITS quantified (time, cost, people, etc.)?
✓ Are there any BONUS BENEFITS to be included?

NEXT STEP

✓ Does the NEXT STEP ask for specific action (requested in the PLAN) by a specific time?

ALIGNMENT CHECKS

1. OBJECTIVE, PLAN, and NEXT STEP
2. NEEDS and RESULTS (benefits)
3. PLAN and HIW

II

The Anatomy of Persuasion® Preparation Guidelines

- *Select a real business or professional persuasion task* on which you wish to make a proposal.

- *Be sure the selected task is both important and timely*—one on which you can take action soon.

- *Define your audience.*

- *Write an objective statement in a clear, concise manner* using no more than fifty words. This statement is your message to you. Its purpose is to define exactly what you want to accomplish with this proposal—and nothing more.

- *Carefully develop the needs* of the person(s) you wish to persuade. Be sure these needs accurately reflect the views of that person. Verify this information with the person involved if possible. Make assumptions about the needs of your audience only when absolutely necessary.

- *Quantify important elements of your proposal.* Develop costs, time, number of people required, quality, quantity, earnings, payback, and so on. In short, be as well informed about your task as possible by knowing the answers to the who, where, what, when, why, how, and how much questions.

III

The Anatomy of Persuasion® Outline Guide

AUDIENCE: Name the person(s) who can act on your proposal.

___

YOUR OBJECTIVE: State exactly what you want to accomplish as a result of this proposal (50 words or less). ___

___

___

NEED(s): Outline your audience's NEEDS as you believe he/she understands them. (Do you have agreement on these needs?)

1) ___

2) ___

3) ___

PLAN: State what you propose that your audience do to satisfy his/her needs (25 words or less).

___

HOW-IT-WORKS: Outline how your PLAN will be carried out.

___

___

RESULTS: Outline what your audience will get in terms of benefits to satisfy his/her needs. (Couple the benefits with the NEEDS listed above.)

1) ___

2) ___

3) ___

NEXT STEP: Request the action you want your audience to take. (Remember: a specific action by a specific time.)

___

Please check your work against the Structure and Alignment Chart.

IV

The Anatomy of Persuasion® Structure and Alignment Chart

Rules of Construction

(1) Write your OBJECTIVE in 50 words or less. Derive your statements of the PLAN and NEXT STEP from your OBJECTIVE. You should have a logical flow of thought from OBJECTIVE through PLAN to NEXT STEP.

(2) The NEEDS of your audience should be completely developed and the RESULTS should translate the NEEDS into appropriate benefits. Be sure to check the sequence.

(3) Your HIW should tell your audience only what it needs to know in principle to understand how your PLAN will be carried out.

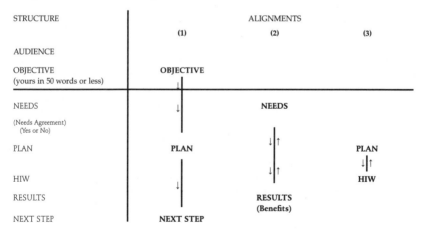

To analyze your proposal, check each of the three alignments separately against the Rules of Construction. When each alignment meets its rule, chances are that the whole proposal will work well when assembled.

Index

[Numbers in italics refer to illustrations. Numbers followed by an *n* refer to footnotes.]